You are my
Grammar &
Speaking

3
Workbook

I am books

Published by

I am Books

#1116, Daeryung Techno Town 12th Bldg.,

14, Gasan digital 2-ro, Geumcheon-gu, Seoul 153-778, Republic of Korea

TEL: 82-2-6343-0999

FAX: 82-2-6343-0995

Visit our website: http://www.iambooks.co.kr

Publishers: Shin Sunghyun, Oh Sangwook

Author: Lucifer EX

Editor: Lee Doohee

Photo Credits:

Wikipedia (www.wikipedia.org): p. 24 (Mars); p. 29 (Thai-style boxing match "Joe Schilling vs. Kaoklai Kaennorsing") © Samuel David Ayres III; p. 99 (blue whale) © Mike Baird from Morro Bay, USA

Flickr (www.flickr.com): p. 30 (Native American "Intertribal Dance") © Tobyotter; p. 59 (Harry Potter Books) © lozikiki; p. 101 (archaeologist "Archaeology at Crossrail") © rich_pickler;

All other photos © imagetoday (www.imagetoday.co.kr)

ISBN: 978-89-6398-096-6 63740

Contents

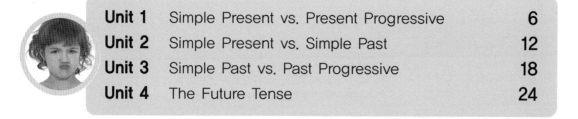

After Finishing the Workbook

Book 3

Teacher's Comments

Parents' Comments

Class

Name

Simple Present vs. Present Progressive

▶ Simple Present vs. Present Progressive
▶ Non-Progressive Verbs
▶ Present Progressive as a Future Tense

Learn & Practice 1

Simple Present vs. Present Progressive

- 현재 시제는 일상적인 습관 또는 반복되는 동작을 나타낼 때 사용해요. 특히 과학적 사실이나 변하지 않는 진리도 현재 시제를 써서 표현해요.

- 현재진행 시제는 말하는 순간, 보고 있는 그 순간에 진행 중인 동작이나 행동을 나타내요. 형태는 'be(am, is, are) + v-ing' 형태를 취하고 우리말로 '~하고 있다, ~하고 있는 중이다'라는 뜻을 가져요.

Simple Present	Present Progressive

 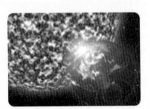 

We **eat** lunch at 1:00 every day.

The earth **moves** around the sun.

That woman **is looking** at me!
She **is wearing** a skirt.
She **is smiling**.

- 현재진행 시제는 최근에 일시적으로 하고 있는 일이나, 긴 시간에 걸쳐 변화하고 있는 동작이나 상태를 나타내요. 최근의 일을 나타낼 때에는 보통 these days, this month, this year, this semester(학기) 등의 표현과 함께 써요.

I'm **working** part-time at a restaurant this month.

The population of the world **is rising** rapidly.

- 현재 시제와 현재진행 시제는 다음과 같은 시간 표현들과 함께 자주 쓰여요.

Simple Present	Present Progressive
Time Expressions	**(Time) Expressions**
every morning/day/week/year, etc.	now, at the moment,
on Monday/Tuesday, etc.	at present, these days, today
in the morning/afternoon/evening	this week/month/year
always, never, sometimes, often, etc.	Look!, Listen!

A Make sentences using the simple present or the present progressive.

1. Kevin / sleep / right now → *Kevin is sleeping right now.*

2. Cindy / not understand / Korean → _____

3. We / work / at my dad's shop / these days → _____

4. Betty / usually / go swimming / on the weekend → _____

5. the teacher / talk / to a student / now → _____

Non-Progressive Verbs

- 동작을 나타내지 않고 어떤 상태가 지속되고 있는 감정, 지각, 소유를 나타내는 동사는 진행형으로 쓸 수 없어요.

The cook **is tasting** the soup.
This soup **tastes** too salty.

Sense	Feeling	Knowledge
hear see smell taste	enjoy feel hate want like love need	think know believe understand remember

- 지속적인 상태를 나타내지 않고 동작을 나타내는 경우에는 동작을 나타내는 진행형을 쓸 수 있어요.

Non-Action Verb	Action in Progress
Karen **has** a sports car. The socks **smell** terrible. They **look** happy.	Karen **is having** lunch. She **is smelling** the socks. They **are looking** out the window.

A Complete the sentences with the correct form of the present progressive or the simple present of the verbs in brackets.

1. I ___know___ (know) it's not your fault.

2. I really _____ (hate) cockroaches.

3. I _____ (think) about breaking up with John.

4. She _____ (look) at me.

5. The cake _____ (taste) too sweet for me.

Present Progressive as a Future Tense

- 어떤 일을 하기로 이미 마음으로 정해 놓은 개인의 일정인 경우에 현재진행형이 미래를 나타낼 수 있어요.
- 주로 움직임을 나타내는 come, go, stay, arrive, leave나 교통수단을 나타내는 fly, walk, ride, drive, take 등이 자주 쓰여요.

Now	Prediction	Future Plan

Please be quiet! I'm speaking on the phone.	Scientists will find a cure for Parkinson's.	Bob is going to Athens next week.

- 개인의 정해진 일정이 아니라, 단순히 미래를 예상하거나 추측할 때에는 진행형 시제를 쓰지 않고 'will + 동사 원형'을 써야 해요.

Ⓐ Look at the pictures and use the prompts make sentences about plans. Use the present progressive.

1.

play soccer / on Sunday

Tom ___is playing soccer on Sunday___ .

2.

go to the movies / tonight

They _____ .

3.

have a party / next weekend

Laura _____ .

4.

fly / to Jeju Island / in two hours

The next plan _____ .

A Look and write what the people usually do and what they are doing now.

1.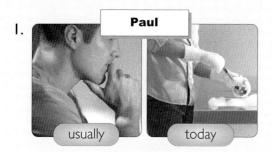
Paul
usually   today

read a book / wash the dishes

→ Paul usually reads a book, but today he is washing the dishes.

2.
Bruno
usually   today

do his homework / play the guitar

→ _____

3.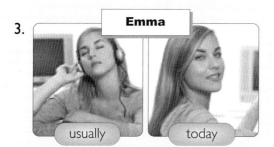
Emma
usually   today

listen to / music / watch a movie on TV

→ _____
_____

4.
Steve
usually   today

take swimming lessons / clean his room

→ _____
_____

B Look at Alice's schedule for next week. Then use the present progressive to make sentences about her plans.

Monday	go to the library to borrow some books
Tuesday	
Wednesday	have lunch with John
Thursday	
Friday	meet her boyfriend
Saturday	see a scary movie with Nick
Sunday	go shopping with her mother

1. Alice is going to the library to borrow some books on Monday.
2. _____
3. _____
4. _____
5. _____

C Make sentences using the simple present or the present progressive.

1. the pizza / taste / good   →   *The pizza tastes good.*

2. the boy / think / about eating a biscuit   → _____

3. what / you / look at?   → _____

4. you / listen to the radio / at the moment?   → _____

5. I / hate / cold evenings   → _____

6. they / look at / clothes at the moment   → _____

7. we / not understand / the lessons   → _____

D Use the prompts below to write questions and answers. Use the simple present or the present progressive.

1.

you / usually / go / fishing / in spring / ?
No → in summer

Q: *Do you usually go fishing in spring?*

A: *No, I don't. I usually go fishing in summer.*

2.

Peter / watch TV / at the moment / ?
No → do the laundry

Q: _____

A: _____

3.

Elena and Jeremy / learn / Chinese / at school / this year / ?
No → Korean

Q: _____

A: _____

4.

Glen / usually / exercise / early / in the morning / ?
No → ride a skateboard

Q: _____

A: _____

A Look at the example and practice with a partner. Use the words below or invent your own. (Then change roles and practice again.)

I.

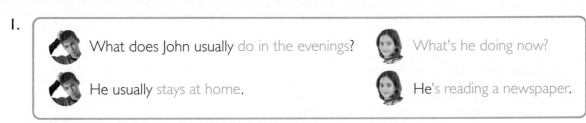

What does John usually do in the evenings?

He usually stays at home.

What's he doing now?

He's reading a newspaper.

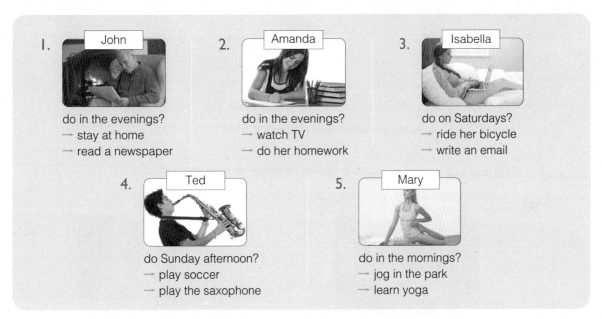

I. **John**
do in the evenings?
→ stay at home
→ read a newspaper

2. **Amanda**
do in the evenings?
→ watch TV
→ do her homework

3. **Isabella**
do on Saturdays?
→ ride her bicycle
→ write an email

4. **Ted**
do Sunday afternoon?
→ play soccer
→ play the saxophone

5. **Mary**
do in the mornings?
→ jog in the park
→ learn yoga

B Work with a partner. Look at the pictures. Ask and answer questions as in the example.

taxi driver / drive a taxi /
wash the taxi

What does the taxi driver do?

He drives a taxi.

Is he driving a taxi now?

No, he isn't. He is washing the taxi.

Your turn to ask now!

vet / treat animals /
listen to music

mechanic / repair cars /
eat a sandwich

nurse / look after patients /
read a book

Simple Present vs. Present Progressive **11**

Simple Present vs. Simple Past

Unit Focus

▶ Simple Present vs. Simple Past
▶ Future: Simple Present
▶ *Used To*: Past Habits

Simple Present vs. Simple Past

- 현재 시제는 반복적으로 일어나는 일이나 행동, 지속적인 상태나 성질을 나타낼 때 써요. 특히 과학적이고 일반적인 사실도 당연히 현재 시제로 나타내요.

- 과거 시제는 과거에 시작하여 과거에 끝나서 현재와는 아무런 상관이 없을 때 써요. 주로 과거의 특정 시간을 나타내는 부사(구)(yesterday, ago, last week, last night, in 1999, in the 1960s 등)와 함께 자주 써요.

- 주어가 3인칭 단수(he, she, mary, a dog, it 등)일 때에만 동사 뒤에 -s나 -es 또는 -ies를 붙여서 현재 시제를 만들어요.

- 과거 시제는 대부분의 동사에 -(e)d를 붙이는데, -ed 또는 -d를 붙이지 않고 불규칙으로 변하는 과거 동사도 있어요.

Tom **eats** lunch.
He **ate** lunch.
He **doesn't** eat lunch.
He **didn't** eat lunch.

Q: **Does** Amy work in the hospital?
A: **Yes**, she does.
Q: **Did** she work yesterday?
A: **No**, she **didn't**.

Affirmative	
I/We/You/They He/She/It	**watch** TV. **watches** TV.
I/We/You/They He/She/It	**watched** TV.

Negative	
I/We/You/They He/She/It	**do not (= don't)** sing. **does not (= doesn't)** sing.
I/We/You/They He/She/It	**did not (= didn't)** sing.

Questions

Does	he/she/it	dance?
Do	you/we/they/I	dance?
Did	I/we/they/you he/she/it	dance?

Q: **Does** he speak English every day?
A: **Yes**, he **does**. / **No**, he **doesn't**.

Q: **Did** they go home at 3:00 yesterday afternoon?
A: **Yes**, they **did**. / **No**, they **didn't**.

A. Make *yes/no* questions and complete the short answers.

1. he / take / a bath every morning

   Q: *Does he take a bath every morning?*   A: No, *he doesn't* .

2. they / live in / Korea 5 years ago

   Q: _____   A: Yes, _____ .

3. she / answer / some emails last night

   Q: _____   A: No, _____ .

4. water / boil / at 100 degrees Celsius

   Q: _____   A: Yes, _____ .

Learn & Practice 2

Future: Simple Present

- 기차, 비행기와 같은 대중교통 시간표나 영화, 연극, 운동 경기 관람 시간과 같이 이미 확실히 정해져 있는 시간표나 일정은 현재 시제로 미래를 나타내요. 주로, arrive, leave, start, begin, end, close, open, finish, be 동사와 자주 쓰여요. 개인의 정해진 일정에는 현재 시제로 미래를 나타내지 않고 현재진행 시제 또는 be going to로 미래를 나타내요.

Q: What time **does** the movie **begin** tomorrow?
A: It **begins** at 10:00 tomorrow morning.

Q: When **does** the train **leave** for Seoul?
A: The first train **leaves** for Seoul at 9:00 a.m.

A. Complete the sentences to talk about action that routinely take place.

1. What time ___*does*___ the train ___*depart*___ on Monday? (depart)

2. When _____ the supermarket _____ today? (close)

3. The train _____ at 9 tomorrow. (arrive)

4. What time _____ your flight _____? (arrive)

5. _____ the plane _____ at 2 or 3 this afternoon? (take off)

Used To: **Past Habits**

- used to는 과거의 반복된 행동이나 지속된 상태를 나타내요. 우리말로 '(과거에) ~하곤 했(었)다'라는 뜻이에요. 지금은 더 이상 하지 않는 과거의 행동(상태)으로 현재와는 아무런 관련이 없는 과거 시제예요.
- 부정은 'didn't use to'를 쓰고 '예전에는 ~하지 않았는데 지금은 ~하다'라는 뜻을 나타내요.
- 의문문은 'Did + 주어 + use to...?'로 쓰고 yes나 no로 대답해요.

Cindy **used to** jog early in the morning.
(Cindy doesn't jog anymore.)

Michelle **didn't use to** wear glasses.
(Michelle wears them now.)

Q: **Did** you **use to** play tennis?
A: **Yes**, I **did**. / **No**, I **didn't**.

Affirmative

| I/We/You He/She/It/They | **used to** | travel. |

Negative

| I/We/You He/She/It/They | **did not** (= **didn't**) | **use to** travel. |

Questions

| **Did** | I/we/you he/she/it/they | **use to** | travel? |

Q: **Did** he **use to** read a lot of books?
A: **Yes**, he **did**. / **No**, he **didn't**.

A Write sentences with the same meaning using *used to* or *didn't use to*.

1. Once she played badminton, but now she doesn't. → *She used to play badminton.*

2. Once Kevin went fishing, but now he doesn't. → _____

3. Once I didn't play the guitar, but now I do. → _____

4. Once we didn't take a taxi, but now we do. → _____

5. Once Claire was lazy, but now she isn't. → _____

6. Once she ate meat, but now she doesn't. → _____

A Look and make sentences as in the example.

every day

Rachel

yesterday

take a shower
drink a lot of milk
brush her teeth
go to school on foot

exercise for an hour
watch her favorite TV show
wash her clothes and dry them
bake cakes for her family

1. Rachel takes a shower every day.

2. Rachel (= She) exercised for an hour yesterday.

3. _____

4. _____

5. _____

6. _____

7. _____

8. _____

B Look at the table and write sentences about Isabella. Use *used to* and *didn't use to*.

Isabella

Three Years Ago	Now
She was a flight attendant.	She is a florist.
She had a boyfriend.	She is single.
She lived in the countryside.	She lives in the city.
She didn't talk much.	She is more outgoing.
She played soccer.	She plays baseball.
She didn't speak much Korean.	She speaks Korean very well.

1. Isabella used to be a flight attendant, but now she is a florist.

2. _____

3. _____

4. _____

5. _____

6. _____

C Look at pictures and prompts. Write questions and answers as in the example.

1.

the flight / leave / at 9:30?
→ No / 11:00

Q: *Does the flight leave at 9:30?*

A: *No, it doesn't. It leaves at 11:00.*

2.

the movie / start / at 9:00?
→ No / 10:00

Q: _____

A: _____

3.

this semester / end / on March 12th?
→ No / March 15th

Q: _____

A: _____

4.

the bank / close / at 3:00 tomorrow
→ No / 5:00

Q: _____

A: _____

D Look at the pictures and read the statements. Then make questions and give short answers.

1.

Q: *Did they walk to the library?*
A: *Yes, they did.* _____ (They walked to the library.)

2.

Q: _____
A: _____ (Kathy talks to John on the phone.)

3.

Q: _____
A: _____ (Jessica doesn't go to the movies.)

4.

Q: _____
A: _____ (The girls stayed at home last night.)

A Look at the example and practice with a partner. Use the words below or invent your own. (Then change roles and practice again.)

1.

1.

Grace / do some exercise
→ listen to K-pop music

 What does Grace usually do every morning?

 She usually does some exercise.

 What did she do this morning?

 She listened to K-pop music.

2.

Sheryl / take a shower
→ take a tennis lesson

3.

Nancy / drink a cup of coffee
→ run along the beach

4.

Tom and Cindy / go to church
→ learn scuba diving

B Work with a partner. Ask and answer questions using the prompts as in the example.

Did you use to bite your nails when you were seven?

No, I didn't. How about you? Did you use to bite your nails?

Yes, I did. Your turn to ask now!

1. listen to fairy tales?
2. watch many cartoons?
3. have a bath every day
4. go to bed late?
5. eat a lot of candies?
6. dress yourself?
7. make your bed?
8. get pocket money?
9. have a different kind of hair style?
10. be afraid of the dark
11. sleep with your parents?
12. live in a foreign country?

Simple Past vs. Past Progressiv

⊛ **Unit Focus**
- ▶ Simple Past vs. Past Progressive
- ▶ Past Progressive: Time Clauses with *While* and *When*
- ▶ Simple Past: Time Clauses with *When*, *Before*, *After*, and *As Soon As*

Learn & Practice 1

Simple Past vs. Past Progressive

- 과거 시제는 이미 과거에 시작한 행동이나 동작이 과거에 끝나 현재와는 아무런 관련이 없어요. 보통 동사에 -(e)d를 붙여서 과거 시제를 만들고 주로 yesterday, last night(week, month, year), ago 등과 함께 자주 쓰여요.
- 과거진행 시제는 과거의 어느 특정한 시간에 어떤 행위가 진행되고 있었음을 나타낼 때 사용해요.

Simple Past	Past Progressive
King Sejong **invented** the Korean alphabet, Hangeul.	 Kevin and Jessica **were riding** a roller coaster at 7:00 yesterday.

Ⓐ **Read the questions and answer them using the prompts.**

1. Did Pablo Picasso live in London? No / in Paris
   → *No, he didn't. He lived in Paris.*

2. Did Marilyn Monroe come from France? No / the United States
   → _____

3. Did Romeo love Cleopatra? No / Juliet
   → _____

4. Did Marie and Pierre Curie discover penicillin? No / radium
   → _____

Ⓑ **Ask *yes/no* questions using the present progressive. Then complete the short answers.**

1. she / write a composition Q: *Was she writing a composition?* A: Yes, *she was* .

2. it / snow last night Q: _____ A: No, _____ .

3. he / study / Spanish Q: _____ A: Yes, _____ .

Past Progressive: Time Clauses with *While* and *When*

- 시간의 접속사와 과거 시제와 과거진행 시제를 함께 쓸 경우, 이미 긴 시간 동안 진행 중이었던 동작은 과거진행 시제를 쓰고 나중에 짧게 일어나 도중에 끼어든 동작은 과거 시제를 써요.
- while과 when이 이끄는 시간의 부사절(time clause)은 중심 문장(main clause)을 보충 설명하는 역할을 하고 단독으로 쓰이면 완전한 문장이 될 수 없어요.

Olivia **was sleeping when** the cell phone **rang** and **woke** her up.

Olivia **was sleeping**. (longer action)
The cell phone **rang** and **woke** her up. (shorter action)

Time Clause	Main Clause
While Alice **was driving** to the bank, **When** the electricity **went off,**	the cell phone **rang**. I **was studying**.
Main Clause	Time Clause
The cell phone **rang** I **was studying**	**while** Alice **was driving** to the bank. **when** the electricity **went off**.

Ⓐ Complete the sentences with the past progressive or the simple past of the verbs in brackets.

1.

arrive / drink

When the email ___arrived___ , she ___was drinking___ the coffee.

2.

watch / knock

I _____ TV when someone _____ at the door.

3.

sit / begin

While we _____ in the park, it suddenly _____ to rain.

Simple Past: Time Clauses with When, Before, After, and As Soon As

- 과거에 먼저 발생한 동작은 과거 시제를 쓰고 연이어 다음 동작이 발생하는 경우에도 과거 시제를 써서 동작의 순서를 나타내요.
- 두 가지 동작이 동시에 진행되고 있었음을 나타낼 때 시간의 부사절과 중심 문장 둘 다 과거진행 시제를 써요.

VS.

When my aunt **arrived**, we **ate** dinner.
(First my aunt arrived. Then we ate dinner.)

When my aunt **arrived**, we **were eating** dinner.
(We had already started dinner.)

VS.

As soon as the light **changed**, a woman **crossed** the street.
(First the light changed. Then she crossed the street.)

While I **was driving**, two girls **were crossing** the street.
(Two actions in progress at the same time.)

Time Clause	Main Clause
As soon as I arrived at the bus stop,	the bus **left**.
Main Clause	Time Clause
The bus **left**	**as soon as I arrived** at the bus stop.

Ⓐ Read each numbered sentence. Write T (True) or F (False) for the statement that follows.

1. When our friends arrived, we ate lunch.
   - Our friends arrived before lunch.   → ___T___

2. While we were talking on the phone, I was driving to school.
   - We finished the conversation. Then I drove to school.   → _____

3. When Mary got to school, her class was taking a test.
   - Mary was late to class.   → _____

4. Joy heard about the accident while she was driving to work.
   - Joy knew about the accident by the time she got to work.   → _____

Super Writing

A Combine the two sentences into one sentence by using time clauses.

1. (before) Main Clause: I peeled it. / Time Clause: I ate the banana.
   → I peeled the banana before I ate it.
   → Before I ate the banana, I peeled it.

2. (when) Main Clause: She was happy. / Time Clause: Bob passed the exam.
   → _____
   → _____

3. (after) Main Clause: He never played soccer again. / Time Clause: He broke his leg.
   → _____
   → _____

4. (as soon as) Main Clause: She went to Namsan Park. / Time clause: She reached Seoul.
   → _____
   → _____

B Look at the pictures and prompts. Write sentences using the simple past or the past progressive and *while* or *when*, as in the example.

1. Sandra / read a novel / I come home / yesterday (when)
   → Sandra was reading a novel when I came home yesterday.

2. Tony / call / you / take a shower (while)
   → _____

3. Nancy and Walter / walk / in the street / it / start / raining (when)
   → _____

4. Elizabeth / watch a drama on TV / her father / arrive (when)
   → _____

5. Ava / ride in a bus / the accident / happen (when)
   → _____

C What were you doing at a specific time? Write one sentence as in the example. The progressive is not always necessary.

1. (at 9:00 last night)   I was listening to K-pop music with my sister.

2. (at this time yesterday)   I was on a bus on my way to class.

3. (at 8:00 yesterday morning) _____

4. (at 10:00 last night) _____

5. (half an hour ago) _____

6. (at this time last year) _____

7. (at 5:00 last Monday) _____

D Look at the following results of different actions. What do you think the person was doing in each situation?

1. She burned her finger.
   (cook)   →   Maybe she was cooking when she burned her finger.

2. He fell off the ladder.
   (change a light bulb)   → _____

3. She heard a strange noise.
   (read a newspaper)   → _____

4. They fell asleep.
   (watch a movie on TV)   → _____

5. She fell down. (go down the stairs without turning on the lights)
   → _____

6. It fell and broke to pieces.
   (He / repair the laptop)   → _____

A Look at the example and practice with a partner. Use the words below or invent your own. (Then change roles and practice again.)

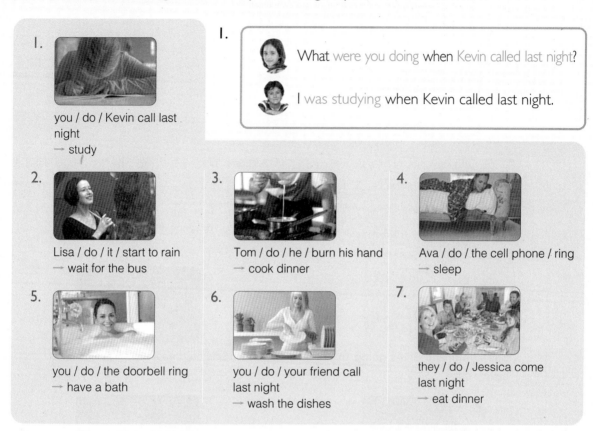

1.

you / do / Kevin call last night
→ study

I.

What were you doing when Kevin called last night?

I was studying when Kevin called last night.

2.

Lisa / do / it / start to rain
→ wait for the bus

3.

Tom / do / he / burn his hand
→ cook dinner

4.

Ava / do / the cell phone / ring
→ sleep

5.

you / do / the doorbell ring
→ have a bath

6.

you / do / your friend call last night
→ wash the dishes

7.

they / do / Jessica come last night
→ eat dinner

B Work with a partner. Combine the two ideas into one sentence to introduce time clauses. Make one sentence with *after* and another with *before*.

They got married.

They had a baby.

After they got married, they had a baby.

Before they had a baby, they got married.

He did some warm-up exercise.

He swam.

She did her homework.

She went to bed.

She saw that horror movie.

She had a nightmare.

Unit **4** **The Future Tense**

Unit Focus

▶ Future: *Be Going To / Will / Be About To*
▶ Future Conditional Sentences
▶ Future Time Clauses with *When*, *Before*, and *After*

Learn & Practice 1

Future: *Be Going To / Will / Be About To*

- be going to는 이미 어떤 일을 하기로 결정되어 있는 미래의 일정(prior plan) 또는 말하는 사람의 마음과 관계없이 눈앞에 뻔히 일어날 상황을 예측할 때 써요.
- will은 앞으로의 일을 단순히 예측하거나, 미래의 일에 대해서 말하는 순간에 결정할 때 사용해요.
- be about to는 몇 분 이내에 일어날 아주 가까운 미래를 표현할 때 쓰고 '막 ~하려고 하다'라고 해석해요.

She's pregnant. She**'s going to** have a baby.

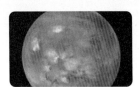

One day people **will travel** to Mars.

Oh no! Eric **is going to** fall into the ground.

Turn off your phone, please. The movie **is about to** start.

Ⓐ Read and Put in *I'll* or *I'm going to*.

1. I've decided. ____*I'm going to*____ stop smoking.

2. A: I don't want to cook tonight. B: All right, then _____ cook.

3. A: Let's oder some pizza. B: Good idea! _____ call.

4. A: Do you have any plans for this weekend? B: Yes, I do. _____ rollerblade with Joe

Ⓑ Complete the sentences using *be about to*.

1. Hurry up! The lesson ____*is about to start*____. (start)

2. I'll call you later. I _____ on a business trip. (go)

3. She has a digital camera. She _____. (take a picture)

24 Unit 4

Future Conditional Sentences

- 조건을 나타내는 부사절 안의 동사는 현재 시제를 써서 미래를 나타내요. 중심 문장(주절)은 조건의 부사절에 대한 결과를 나타내는 역할을 해요. 의미가 미래를 나타내더라도 조건의 부사절에는 미래를 나타내는 will과 be going to를 쓰지 않아요.

- 'If + 주어 + 동사…'만으로 완전한 문장을 만들 수 없고 반드시 중심 문장과 함께 써야 의미를 전달할 수 있어요. 중심 문장 앞, 또는 뒤에 모두 쓸 수 있고, if가 이끄는 절이 문장의 앞에 올 때에는 쉼표(,)를 써요.

If I **go** on a diet, **I'll lose** weight.

We**'re going to** play badminton if it **doesn't rain**.

- 일반적인 사실, 일상적으로 일어나는 일이나 정해진 상황을 가정할 때에는 if절과 주절에 모두 현재 시제를 써요.

If people **sneeze**, they **close** their eyes.

She **sleeps** for the rest of the afternoon if nobody **disturbs** her.

A Complete the sentences with the right form of the verbs in brackets.

1.

Her boss ___shouts___ (shout) at her if he sees her speaking on the phone.

2.

If he _____ (not feed) the kitten, they will go hungry.

3.

Karen _____ (fail) the math exam if she doesn't make an effort.

4.

If the temperature of water _____ (drop) to freezing point, it turns into ice.

Future Time Clauses with When, Before, and After

- 시간의 부사절이 미래의 의미를 나타내더라도 시간의 부사절 안의 동사는 반드시 현재 시제를 써서 미래를 나타내요. 미래 시제 will 또는 be going to를 쓰지 않아요.
- 시간의 부사절은 중심 문장(main clause)과 반드시 함께 써야 완전한 의미를 전달할 수 있어요. 중심 문장 앞에 또는 뒤에 쓸 수 있고 접속사(when, after, before)가 이끄는 절이 문장의 앞에 올 때에는 쉼표(,)를 써요.

I'll give him a hug when he **comes** out of the gate.

Before Nancy **gets** on the plane, she **will go** to the duty-free shop.

- 일반적인 사실, 일상적으로 일어나는 일이나 정해진 상황을 가정할 때에는 시간의 부사절과 주절에 모두 현재 시제를 써요.

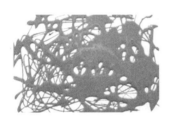

When you **mix** yellow and blue, you **get** green.

After Olivia **finishes** her work, she always **plays** the piano.

Ⓐ Complete the sentences with the right form of the verbs in brackets.

1. Ice ___melts___ (melt) when you ___heat___ (heat) it. `truth`

2. When it _____ (get) dark in the desert, it _____ (get) cold. `truth`

3. After Megan _____ (get) to work, she _____ (listen) to music. `habit`

4. Before I _____ (go) home, I _____ (buy) the scarf at the store. `future`

5. When my sister _____ (turn) 29 next year, she _____ (get) married. `future`

6. When you _____ (take) fish out of the water, they _____ (die). `truth`

A Look at Steve's list of appointments for Tuesday and write sentences using *be going to*. Use the verbs in the box.

attend	fly	give	have	meet

TUESDAY

10:00 his bank manager
1:00 lunch with Susan
2:00 an interview at an NBC studio
4:00 Japan - Incheon International Airport
6:00 the Music Monthly Awards Ceremony

1. He's going to meet his bank manager at 10 o'clock.
2. _____
3. _____
4. _____
5. _____

B Look at the pictures and expand the notes into sentences. Use the words given and time clauses.

1.  **when**

I / have / a cup of coffee / I / get home / tonight

→ I will have a cup of coffee when I get home tonight.

2.   **after**

Peter and Ava / go to the movie theater / they / have lunch

→ _____

3.  **before**

they / wash the car / they / watch / their favorite show on TV

→ _____

4.   **when**

I / get married / I / be 27 years old

→ _____

The Future Tense **27**

C Complete the sentences with either *be going to* or *will*.

1. A: Why did you go to Seoul? (Speaker B is planning to attend a meeting from 9:00 to 10:00.)
   B: I ____*am going to*____ attend a meeting from 9:00 to 10:00.

2. A: Could someone get me a glass of water? (Speaker B doesn't have a plan.)
   B: Certainly. I _____ get you one. Would you like some ice in it?

3. A: Oh no! I wasn't watching the time. I missed my school bus. (Speaker B doesn't have a plan.)
   B: That's Okay. I _____ give you a ride home.

4. A: Do you have a car? (Speaker B is planning to sell his car.)
   B: Yes, but I _____ sell it. I don't need it now that I live in the city.

D Combine the ideas of the two sentences into one sentence by using an *if*-clause.

> **POSSIBLE CONDITION** ⟶ **RESULT**

1. Maybe it will rain tomorrow. ⟶ I'm going to stay home.
   ⟶ *If it rains tomorrow, I'm going to stay home. / I'm going to stay home if it rains tomorrow.*
   _____

2. Maybe you won't learn how to use a computer. ⟶ You will have trouble finding a job.
   ⟶ _____

3. Maybe John will do well in science. ⟶ His parents will buy him a smartphone.
   ⟶ _____

4. Maybe we will leave now. ⟶ We will probably get caught in traffic.
   ⟶ _____

E Look at the pictures. Complete the sentences using *be about to* as in the example.

1.

   He ____*is about to kick the ball.*____ .
   (kick the ball)

2.

   They _____ .
   (eat at a mall)

3.

   Ryan _____ .
   (do the launday)

4.

   Lisa _____ .
   (open the window)

A Look at the example and practice with a partner. Use the words below or invent your own. (Then change roles and practice again.)

1.

go / downtown tomorrow
→ buy a new coat

1.

 Maybe you'll go downtown tomorrow.

 If I go downtown tomorrow, I'll buy a new coat.

2.

finish / your homework
→ take a walk

3.

be tired / tonight
→ stay at home

4.

not be tired / tonight
→ go / to a movie

5.

have / enough time
tomorrow
→ go on a hike

6.

not study tonight
→ not pass the exam

7.

go / to Bangkok
→ watch a Thai-style boxing
match

B Which of the following events do you think will happen in the future? Check your answers and then discuss.

	Agree	Disagree
1. There will be less pollution and no more disease.		
2. There will be no more wars.		
3. We'll travel around the world in an hour by space shuttle.		
4. There will be no more schools because children will learn at home through the Internet.		
5. There will be a single government for the entire world.		
6. There will be no more offices. Everyone will work from home.		
7. Twenty years from now, there will be fewer trees in our city.		

Unit 5 Quantifying Expressions

Unit Focus
▶ A Few / Few vs. A Little / Little
▶ Many, Much, A Lot Of / Lots Of
▶ Too Many/Much vs. A Lot Of

Learn & Practice 1

A Few / Few vs. A Little / Little

- a few는 셀 수 있는 명사 앞에서 많지 않은 수, a little은 셀 수 없는 명사 앞에서 많지 않은 양을 나타내요. a few는 '조금의, 몇 개의'라고 해석하고, a little은 '약간의'라는 뜻으로 해석해요.
- few는 셀 수 있는 명사 앞에서 '거의 없는 (수)'이라는 부정의 의미고, little 또한 셀 수 없는 명사 앞에서 '거의 없는 (양)'이라는 부정의 의미를 담고 있어요.

A Few / Few + Plural Countable Nouns	A Little / Little + Uncountable Nouns
 Scott drinks **a few** glasses of juice every day.	 Do you want **a little** milk in your coffee?
 (Very) **Few** young Native Americans speak the language of their ancestors.	 When there is (very) **little** rain, plants can't grow.

- very를 few 또는 little 앞에 써서 부정의 의미를 더욱 강조하기도 해요.

A Complete the sentences with *a few, few, a little* or *little*.

1. Only ___a few___ children like math because it is so hard to understand.

2. We don't think Mrs. Wilson would be a good teacher. She has _____ patience with children.

3. There was _____ traffic, so I arrived earlier than I expected.

4. The weather isn't very good. There are very _____ people at the beach.

5. I must go shopping. There is _____ food in the fridge.

6. She was not very late, just _____ minutes late for the meeting.

Many, Much, A Lot Of / Lots Of

- many는 셀 수 있는 명사 앞, much는 셀 수 없는 명사 앞에서 정확한 수나 양을 알 수는 없지만 막연히 '많은'이라는 뜻을 나타내요. 셀 수 없는 명사는 그 양이 아무리 많아도 단수 취급하여 동사도 단수 동사를 써야 해요.
- a lot of와 lots of는 '많은'이라는 뜻으로 셀 수 있는 명사와 셀 수 없는 명사 앞에 모두 쓸 수 있어요.
- many와 a lot of는 긍정문, 부정문, 의문문에 모두 쓰지만, much는 긍정문에 잘 사용하지 않고 주로 부정문과 의문문에 써요.
- how many와 how much는 '얼마나'라는 뜻으로, 그 수와 양을 물어보는 말이에요. how many 뒤에는 셀 수 있는 복수 명사를 쓰고, how much 뒤에는 셀 수 없는 명사를 써요.

I have **many** friends.

Do you drink **much** coffee?

I usually have **a lot of** homework.

A Read and choose the correct words.

1. Are there (much / (a lot of)) people in the swimming pool?

2. There aren't (much / many) books on the shelf.

3. How (much / a lot of) sugar do you need?

4. There is (many / a lot of) milk in the carton.

5. This sweater doesn't cost (many / much) money.

6. Did you prepare (a lot of / many) food for Thanksgiving?

B Write questions with *how many* or *how much* as in the example.

1. apples / you / eat / every day?
   → How many apples do you eat every day?

2. milk / you / drink / every day?
   → _____

3. books / you / buy / every month?
   → _____

Too Many/Much vs. A Lot Of

- too many는 셀 수 있는 명사 앞에서 지나치게 많은 수, too much는 셀 수 없는 명사 앞에서 지나치게 많은 양을 나타내요.
- a lot of는 단순히 '많은'이라는 뜻을 나타내지만 too many와 too much는 너무 많아서 문제가 있다는 어감을 내포하고 있어요.

She reads **a lot of** books.
She even reads on the beach.

There are **too many** cars on the road. We won't get to the reception on time.

Ava eats **too much** fast food. She should eat more fruit and vegetables.

A **Complete the sentences with *too many* or *too much*.**

1. Mr. Kevin spent ____*too much*____ money on the party.

2. There were _____ guests and _____ food.

3. There were _____ flowers everywhere.

4. A: I don't like this parking lot. Let's leave.
   B: What's wrong with you?
   A: There are _____ cars, and there is _____ smoke in here.

5. A: You bought _____ oranges at the market yesterday.
   B: Never mind, we can use some for juice.

6. A: How did you spoil the soup?
   B: I put _____ salt in it.

7. A: I don't like this coffee.
   B: Why not?
   A: There's _____ sugar in it.

A Look at the pictures. Make questions with *many* or *much* and then complete the answers with *(a) few*, *(a) little*, or *any*.

1.

doughnut

Q: Are there many doughnuts on the plate?

A: No, there are a few doughnuts (on the plate).

2.

butter

Q: _____

A: No, _____

3.

money

Q: _____

A: No, _____

4.

cheese

Q: _____

A: No, _____

5.

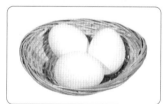

egg

Q: _____

A: No, _____

6.

cookie

Q: _____

A: No, _____

7.

tomato

Q: _____

A: No, _____

8.

milk

Q: _____

A: No, _____

B Make questions with *how many* or *how much*. Use the information in parentheses to form each question.

1. Q: How many students are there in your class? _____

   A: Twenty. (There are twenty students in my class.)

2. Q: _____

   A: A lot. (I took a lot of suntan oil with me.)

3. Q: _____

   A: A lot. (There is a lot of milk in the fridge.)

4. Q: _____

   A: Eleven. (There are eleven players on a soccer team.)

C Change *a lot of* to *too many* or *too much*. Use *too many* with plural countable nouns. Use *too much* with singular uncountable nouns.

1. Matt has a lot of problems.   →   Kevin has too many problems. _____

2. There is a lot of food on the table.   →   _____

3. Anna buys a lot of fruit at the market. →   _____

4. There are a lot of cars in the city center. →   _____

D Use the prompts and write sentences with *a few*, *a little*, and *any*, as in the example.

1. cherries / fridge   → X appples

   There are a few cherries in the fridge, but there aren't any apples. _____

2. bananas / fridge   → X oranges

   _____

3. milk / fridge   → X yogurt

   _____

4. ice cream / fridge   → X chocolate

   _____

5. potatoes / fridge   → X carrots

   _____

A Look at the example and practice with a partner. Use the words below or invent your own. (Then change roles and practice again.)

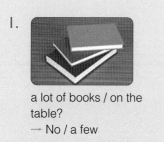

1.
a lot of books / on the table?
→ No / a few

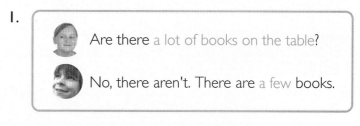

1.
Are there a lot of books on the table?

No, there aren't. There are a few books.

2.
many students / in the library?
→ No / a few

3.
much bread / in the plate?
→ No / a little

4.
much food / in the fridge
→ No / little

5.
a lot of coins / in her hand?
→ No / a few

6.
many ducks / in the lake?
→ No / a few

7.
a lot of salt / on the cutting board?
→ No / a little

B Work with a partner. Ask questions with *how many* or *how much*. Circle the appropriate answers and add up your partner's score.

More As?	More Bs?	More Cs?
You need to be more careful. You spend too much money.	Good for you! You won't have any money problems.	You need to enjoy life more. Don't be afraid to spend a little money.

How much money do you spend on clothes?

A lot of money.

1. money / you / spend / on clothes?
   a. A lot of money.
   b. A little money.
   c. No money at all.

2. movies / you / see / a month?
   a. A lot of movies.
   b. Once a month.
   c. I never see movies.

3. books / you / buy / every week?
   a. Lots of books.
   b. Only a few books.
   c. I don't buy any books.

4. money / you / spend / when / you / go out?
   a. Lots of money.
   b. I don't spend much money.
   c. I never go out.

Unit 6 Expressions of Quantity

Unit Focus
- ▶ *All*, *Almost All Of*, *Most Of*, and *Some Of*
- ▶ Expressions of Quantity: Subject-Verb Agreement
- ▶ *One Of*, *None Of*

Learn & Practice 1

All, Almost All Of, Most Of, and *Some Of*

- all, almost all, most, some 뒤에 특정하지 않은 일반적인 명사(general nouns)가 오면 of를 쓰지 않고, 특정한 명사 (specific nouns)가 오면 of를 써야 해요. 특정한 명사란, 명사 앞에 the, this, that, these, those, my, your, his 등으 로 가리키는 것이 정해진 명사를 말해요.

- all은 뒤에 특정 명사가 오더라도 of를 써도 되고, 안 써도 돼요(all my friends, all of the friends, all the friends 등). 하지만, all 뿐만 아니라 almost all, most, some도 명사가 대명사일 경우에는 반드시 of를 써야 해요(all of it, all of them, almost all of them, some of us등).

All						
Almost All Of						
Most Of						
Some Of						

All students must have an ID card. (General)
Most of them are girls. (Specific)
All (of) the students are looking at their teacher. (Specific)

Almost all of them are sitting. (Specific)
Some of them are boys. (Specific)

A Complete the sentences with *all* or *all of*.

1. ___All___ children like to play soccer.

2. _____ the children like to play soccer.

3. _____ cities have the same problems.

4. _____ animals need oxygen like human beings.

5. _____ them speak excellent English.

B Complete the sentences with *of* or with X.

1. Some ___X___ people don't like vegetables.

2. Some _____ my books are in English.

3. Almost of all _____ them are standing.

4. Most _____ the people come from Korea.

5. Most _____ men and women apply for that job.

6. Almost all _____ people dislike paying taxes.

Expressions of Quantity: Subject-Verb Agreement

- 주어가 수량을 나타내는 all (of), some (of), almost all (of), most (of)와 함께 쓰일 때에는 주어로 쓰인 명사에 따라 동사의 단수, 복수를 일치시켜야 해요. 다시 말해서, 명사가 단수이면 단수 동사, 복수이면 동사도 복수 동사로 일치시켜야 해요. of로 연결될 때에는 of 뒤에 있는 명사에 따라 동사의 수를 일치시켜요.

All the **people** in the photo **are** students.
(*People* is plural, so the verb is plural.)

All the **food is** delicious.
(*Food* is singular, so the verb is singular.)

All of the **children are** playing soccer.
(*Children* is plural, so the verb is plural.)

Almost all of the **air** in the city is polluted.
(*Air* is singular, so the verb is singular.)

Most of the **residents are** Christian.
(*Residents* is plural, so the verb is plural.)

Some of the **fruit is** rotten.
(*Fruit* is singular, so the verb is singular.)

A Read and circle the correct verb.

1. All the dishes (**come** / comes) with a salad.

2. All of the windows (is / are) open.

3. Most of the apples in the basket (is / are) green.

4. Most of the river (has / have) dried up.

5. Almost all of the furniture (is / are) Italian.

6. Some of the girls (is / are) wearing red shorts.

7. Some of my homework (is / are) finished.

One Of, None Of

- one of는 '~의 하나'라는 의미로 of 뒤에는 반드시 특정 명사(the/those/these/my/your...+ noun)가 와요. 명사는 반드시 복수 명사를 써야 해요. 'one of + 복수 명사'가 주어로 쓰일 때에는 one이 주어이면서 단수 명사이므로 동사도 단수 동사를 써요.

- none of는 그 자체가 '~중 아무도(한 사람도) ~않다'라는 부정의 의미를 담고 있어서 동사를 부정문으로 만들지 않고 긍정문으로만 써야 해요. of 뒤에 있는 특정 명사가 주어이고 반드시 복수 명사를 씁니다. 주어가 복수 명사임에도 불구하고 동사는 단수, 복수 둘 다 쓸 수 있어요.

One Of + Plural Noun

Coffee is **one of** foreign **imports**.

One Of + Plural Noun + Singular Verb

One of my favorite sports **is** curling.

None Of + Plural Noun + Singular Verb

None of the students **speaks** Japanese.

None Of + Plural Noun + Plural Verb

None of them **are** wearing hats.

Ⓐ Complete the sentences with *one of* or *none of*.

1.

   None of them are teachers.

2.

   _____ them is tall.

3.

   _____ the students are boys.

4.

   _____ them is a teacher.

A Look at the picture and complete the sentences with *all the*, *most of the*, *almost all of the*, *some of the*, *one of the*, or *none of the*.

1. _____All (of) the people_____ are outside.

2. _____ are sitting.

3. _____ are students.

4. _____ are smiling.

5. _____ is a teacher.

6. _____ are wearing glasses.

7. _____ are girls.

8. _____ isn't looking at the teacher.

9. _____ is wearing hats.

10. _____ are wearing jeans.

11. _____ are wearing school uniforms.

B Answer these questions using *all of them* or *none of them*, as in the example.

1. Q: Are Robert Downey, Jr., Brad Pitt, and Johnny Depp singers?

   A: No, none of them is/are singers. _____

2. Q: Are cows, goats, and pigs wild animals?

   A: _____

3. Q: Are Korea, Japan, and China countries?

   A: _____

4. Q: Are snakes, tigers, and elephants farm animals?

   A: _____

5. Q: Are Hugh Jackman, Gwyneth Paltrow, and Lee Byunghun movie stars?

   A: _____

C Make sentences from the given words and phrases.

1. almost all of / the students in Korea / study / English / in elementary school
   → *Almost all of the students in Korea study English in elementary school.*

2. one of / my favorite soccer players / be / Park Jisung
   → _____

3. none of / those bags / be / mine
   → _____

4. most of / the information / be / useless
   → _____

5. none of / the students / in my class / speak / Korean
   → _____

6. almost all of the / air / in the city / be / polluted
   → _____

D Rewrite the sentences as in the example.

1. My family all like traveling.   → *All my family like traveling.*
2. The buses all run on Sundays.   → _____
3. The movies all start at 6 o'clock.   → _____
4. The lessons all will start on Tuesday. → _____
5. The shops will all be open tomorrow. → _____

E Look at the pictures. Use the prompts to write sentences. Use *all or none + of them*.

1.
   have / long hair: *All of them have long hair.*
   short hair: *None of them have/has short hair.*

2.
   live / in Africa: _____
   in Europe: _____

3.
   be / in Korea: _____
   in Japan: _____

A Look at the example and practice with a partner. Use the words below or invent your own. (Then change roles and practice again.)

1.

people / be / women?
→ all of

1.

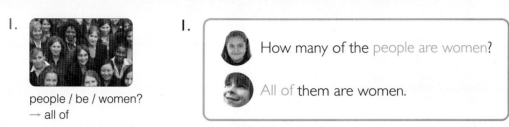

How many of the people are women?

All of them are women.

2.

people / be enjoying
the movie?
→ none of

3.

girls / be wearing
dresses
→ all of

4.

people / be sitting
→ some of

5.

the windows / be /
open?
→ none of

6.

the workers / be looking at
the camera?
→ one of

B Work with a partner. Look at the TV programs below. Make questions and answer them about your classmates.

How many of your classmates like soap operas?

Almost all of them like soap operas.

Your turn to ask now!

reality shows							all (of)
soap operas							almost all of
sports programs							most of
cartoons							some of
the news							one of
the weather forecast							none of
wildlife documentaries							some of

Very, Too, and *Enough*

▶ *Very* and *Too*
▶ *Too* + Adjective (*For* + Noun) + Infinitive
▶ Adjective + *Enough* (+ Infinitive) / *Enough* + Noun

Learn & Practice 1

Very and *Too*

- very와 too는 둘 다 형용사 앞에 쓰여서 우리말로 '너무(아주) ~한'이라는 뜻을 나타내요. 둘 다 뒤에 있는 형용사를 강조하는 역할을 해요.
- very와 too의 뜻은 같지만 서로 약간의 차이가 있어요. very는 '어려움이나 문제가 있지만 가능하다'는 의미를 나타내고, too는 '어려움이나 문제가 있어 불가능하다'는 의미를 내포하고 있어요.

Very + Adjective	*Too* + Adjective

The car was **very** expensive, but she decided to buy it.	The baggage is **too** heavy. Phil can't carry it.

A Complete the sentences with *too* or *very*.

1. The chair is _____very_____ heavy, but she can carry it.

2. The teacher's voice is _____ quiet. We can't understand her.

3. The weather is _____ hot, but the breeze keeps us cool.

4. It's _____ noisy in the house. I can't sleep.

5. We failed the test. It was _____ difficult.

B Complete the sentences. Use the expressions from the box.

go swimming	buy it	forgive him	eat it

1. The food is too hot. We can't _____*eat it*_____.

2. Ella is too tired. She can't _____.

3. The used car is too damaged. Bill can't _____.

4. Monica is too angry. She will never _____.

Too + Adjective (For + Noun) + Infinitive

- 부정사는 동사 앞에 to를 붙여 동작의 표현을 늘리기 위해서 만든 것으로서 우리말로 '~하는 것, ~하기, ~하기에' 등의 뜻으로 쓰여요. 특정한 상황에서 부정적인 결과를 낳는 'too + adjective' 뒤에 부정사를 쓰면 '~하기에 너무 ~하다'라는 뜻이 돼요. 즉, '~하기에'라는 동작을 나타내는 부정사가 형용사를 꾸며 주는 역할을 한답니다.

- 부정사는 '동작, 행동'을 나타내는데 실제 그 행위를 하는 주인(주체)을 명확히 나타내고자 할 때에는 부정사 바로 앞에 'for + 명사 / 목적격 대명사'로 그 동작에 대한 주어를 표시해 줄 수 있어요. 문장에서 실질적인 주어는 아니지만 부정사가 행하는 동작에 대한 주어 역할만을 해요.

These jeans are **too big**. I can't wear them.

These jeans are **too big to wear**.

These jeans are **too big** *for me* **to wear**.

＊부정사 뒤에 부정사의 목적어인 대명사를 쓰면 안 돼요. (These jeans are too big for me to wear them.)

Ⓐ Make one sentence from the two sentences. Use *too* + adjective + *for* pronoun + infinitive.

1.

The motorcycle is too expensive. I can't buy it.

→ *The motorcycle is too expensive for me to buy.*

2.

The water is too dirty. We can't drink it.

→ _____

3.

Steve is too young. He can't drive a car.

→ _____

4.

It is too noisy. I can't sleep.

→ _____

Adjective + *Enough* (+ Infinitive) / *Enough* + Noun

- enough는 형용사가 나오면 형용사 뒤에 쓰고 명사가 나오면 그 앞에 써요. 각각 '충분한, 충분히'라는 뜻으로 긍정의 의미를 담고 있어요.
- enough가 부정문과 함께 쓰일 때에는 어려움이 있어서 불가능한 일을 나타내요.
- '형용사 + enough + to 부정사'에서 부정사는 우리말로 '~할 정도로'라는 뜻이 되고, 'enough + 명사 + to 부정사'에서 부정사는 우리말 '~할'이라는 뜻으로 해석하여 앞에 있는 명사를 꾸며 줘요.

Adjective + *Enough*	Enough + Noun

The meal isn't **cheap enough**. (= The meal is too expensive.)	Some children don't eat **enough vegetables**.

Jessica is **old enough to** travel alone. (= She can travel alone.)	I have **enough time to** go to the movie theater.

A Circle the correct order.

1. She is (pretty enough / enough pretty) to be an actress.

2. He is (smart enough / enough smart) to solve this problem.

3. We have (money enough / enough money) to buy a computer.

4. The ladder is not (enough tall / tall enough) for the man.

5. She is (enough strong / strong enough) to carry the box.

6. They had (time enough / enough time) to go to the park.

7. There aren't (enough chairs / chairs enough) for everybody to sit down.

A Look at the pictures and read the sentences. Write sentences using *too* or *enough* and the words given.

1.

Jason can't buy that house. (expensive)

It is too expensive.

2.

Kevin doesn't like this cafe. (crowded)

_____

3.

Eric can't play basketball well. (not tall)

_____

4.

Sarah can't make a chocolate cake. (not have chocolate)

_____

B Use the prompts in brackets to complete the sentences. Use *too* or *enough* + an infinitive.

1. (strong / move)   She's not ___strong enough to move___ the piano.

2. (tired / go)   I am _____ to the movies.

3. (heavy / carry)   The suitcase is _____.

4. (tall / touch)   He isn't _____ the ceiling.

5. (hot / drink)   This coffee is _____.

6. (full / hold)   My suitcase is _____ any more clothes.

7. (smart / understand) John is _____ how to solve that problem.

C A person is complaining about the school cafeteria. Write sentences using the words in brackets and *too* or *enough*.

1. The water is (hot). It is not (cold).   →   The water is too hot. It is not cold enough.

2. The waiter is (rude). He isn't (polite).   →   _____

3. The plate is (dirty). It isn't (clean).   →   _____

4. The meat is (tough). It isn't (tender).   →   _____

5. The food is (expensive). It isn't (cheap).   →   _____

D Make sentences for each picture. Use *very* or *too* and *can* or *can't* to describe the pictures.

1.

| Ava | Sophie |

the baggage / heavy / lift

→ The baggage is very heavy, but Ava can lift it.

→ The baggage is too heavy. Sophie can't lift it.

2.

| Julie | Laura |

the jeans / tight / wear

→ _____

→ _____

3.

| Kate | Eric |

the shoes / big / wear

→ _____

→ _____

4.

| Alice | Sarah |

the car / expensive / buy

→ _____

→ _____

E Write questions and answers using the words and phrases given.

1. time / go to the park

Q: Do you have enough time to go to the park?

A: No (Yes), I don't have (have) enough time to go to the park.

2. money / to buy a diamond ring

Q: _____

A: _____

3. time / to finish your homework

Q: _____

A: _____

4. vegetables / to make five sandwiches

Q: _____

A: _____

A Look at the example and practice with a partner. Use the words below or invent your own. (Then change roles and practice again.)

I.

Susan / lift / the baggage?
→ too heavy

1.

Why can't Susan lift the baggage?

She can't lift it because it is too heavy.

2.

Julia / buy / the T-shirt?
→ too small

3.

Jennifer / watch the end of the movie on TV?
→ too sleepy

4.

Sam / go to the movie theater?
→ too busy

B Work with a partner. Can you and your partner change these sentences? Make sentences with the same meaning.

1. The baby is only four years old. He can't read and write. (too)

2. You can read this book. The story is interesting. (enough)

3. This hat is too big. Kelly can't wear it. (too)

4. Mary's English is not good. She can't get a job. (enough)

5. We can't go swimming today. It is very cold. (too)

6. Jessica can win the beauty contest. She is very beautiful. (enough)

7. Sally can't buy those shoes. They are too expensive. (too)

The baby is too young to read and write. Your turn now!

Unit Focus

▶ Somebody/Anybody, Something/Anything, Somewhere/Anywhere
▶ Nobody, Nothing, Nowhere
▶ One/Ones

Learn & Practice 1

Somebody/Anybody, Something/Anything, Somewhere/Anywhere

- 부정대명사(indefinite pronouns)는 정해져 있지 않은 명사를 대신하여 쓰는 대명사예요.

- somebody는 잘 알지 못하는 사람, something은 잘 알지 못하는 사물, somewhere는 잘 알지 못하는 장소를 가리키고, 이 세 가지 모두 긍정문에 주로 사용해요.

- 의문문과 부정문에는 주로 각각 anybody, anything, anywhere를 써서 잘 알지 못하는 사람, 사물, 장소를 나타내요.

Affirmative	Negative	Question

This is strange. There's **something** wrong. The door is open.	I'm tired. I don't want to go **anywhere** today.	Do you know **anything** about computers?

	Affirmative Statements	Negative Statements	Questions
Unknown People	somebody (= someone)	anybody (= anyone)	anybody (= anyone)
Unknown Things	something	anything	anything / *something
Unknown Places	somewhere	anywhere	anywhere

＊미국 영어에서는 *someone, anyone*보다 *somebody, anybody*를 더 자주 써요. *something*은 권유나 요구를 나타낼 때 의문문에서도 쓸 수 있어요.

There isn't **anybody** (= **anyone**) at school.　　There is **somebody** (= **someone**) at the door.
Is there **anybody** at the door?　　Would you like to have ***something** to drink?
I'm not going **anywhere**.　　I put my glasses **somewhere**, and now I can't find them.

- 부정대명사를 주어로 쓸 때에는 반드시 동사는 3인칭 단수형을 써야 해요.

Somebody **is** in my room.　　**Is** there anybody here?

A Choose the correct words.

1. I didn't go (anywhere / somewhere) yesterday.

2. Did you see (somebody / anybody) at the park?

3. She didn't receive (something / anything) from her boyfriend on her birthday.

4. We saw (someone / anybody) in the dark room.

5. Did you go (anywhere / somewhere) interesting for your holidays?

6. Did you meet (somebody / anybody) interesting at the party?

Learn & Practice 2

Nobody, Nothing, Nowhere

- nobody(=no one)는 사람, nothing은 사물, nowhere는 장소 전체를 부정하는 대명사예요. '누구도/무엇도 ~아니다'라는 뜻이고 긍정문과 의문문에 쓰여요.

- nobody, nothing, nowhere는 자체가 부정의 의미이므로 부정 동사를 쓰면 안 돼요. 부정문을 만들려면 nothing은 'not + anything', nobody(= no one)는 'not + anyone'으로 바꿔 부정문을 만들어요.

I know **nothing** about the accident.
= I **don't** know **anything** about the accident.

I'm lonely. I have **nobody** to talk to.
= I **don't** have **anybody** to talk to.

＊부정대명사를 주어로 쓸 때 동사는 단수 동사를 써요. (E.g. Nobody likes her.)

	Affirmative Statements	Negative Statements	Questions
Unknown People	nobody (= no one)		nobody (= no one)
Unknown Things	nothing		nothing
Unknown Places	nowhere		nowhere

A Write *nobody*, *nothing*, or *nowhere*.

1. It's too dark. I can't see anything. → It's too dark. I can see ___nothing___.

2. I don't know anybody in neighborhood. → I know _____ in neighborhood.

3. There isn't anywhere to go. → There is _____ to go.

4. He didn't buy anything yesterday. → He bought _____ yesterday.

One/Ones

- one은 단수 명사, ones는 복수 명사를 대신할 때 쓰는 대명사예요. 종류는 같지만 대상이 다른 경우에 명사의 반복을 피하기 위해서 써요.
- one과 ones는 셀 수 없는 명사를 대신하는 대명사로 쓰지 않아요. (E.g. water, cheese 등)
- 이미 앞에서 언급되어 바로 그것(똑같은 대상)을 나타낼 때에는 it, they, them으로 명사의 반복을 피해요.

A: Do you like the yellow **scarf**?
B: No. I like this **one**.

I don't like the red **roses**, but I like the white **ones**.

My sister has a sports **car**, but she doesn't like **it**.

Nick bought some **flowers** and gave **them** to his mother.

A Complete the sentences with *one* or *it*.

1. A: Do you have an idea? B: Yes, I have __one__ .

2. Here comes the taxi. Let's catch _____ .

3. I saw the movie. _____ was great.

B Complete the sentences with *one*, *ones*, *it*, or *them*.

1. A: Does anyone have a dictionary? B: I have __one__ .

2. My dog gave birth to two puppies yesterday. I like _____ very much.

3. I am throwing away the old magazines and keeping the new _____ .

4. I don't have a pencil. Can you lend me _____ ?

5. I'm sorry, but I broke this glass. I dropped _____ .

A Complete the sentences. Choose one of the words in the box.

something	anybody	nowhere	anything
anywhere	nobody	somebody	somewhere

1. This bag is empty. There isn't ___anything___ in it.

2. I'm lonely. I have _____ to talk to.

3. She said _____, but I didn't understand her.

4. Did you go _____ interesting for your vacation?

5. Q: What are you doing here? A: I'm waiting for _____.

6. It's a secret. Don't tell _____.

7. We don't go out very much because there's _____ to go.

8. They live _____ in the south of France.

B Rewrite the following sentences using *one* or *ones*.

1.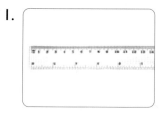

Do you want the long rulers or the short rulers?

→ Do you want the long rulers or the short ones?

2.

We threw away the old sofa and bought a new sofa.

→ _____

3.

That car is fast but this car is faster.

→ _____

4.

This plate is too small. Please get me a bigger plate.

→ _____

5.

This story is as interesting as the other stories.

→ _____

6.

I don't want the blue pen. Please give me the red pen.

→ _____

C The underlined words are incorrect. Correct and rewrite the essay.

Abby is going to a party on Friday, but she has anything to wear. She went to the big clothing store near her home yesterday but didn't find something nice. This morning she went anywhere else, but everything was expensive. At another shop, everything was nice, but anything would fit her. There's anywhere else to go. Abby is going to look in her wardrobe and find anything to wear to the party.

➡

Abby is going to a party on Friday, but she has nothing to wear.

D Rewrite these sentences using *one* or *ones*.

1. This dress is too small for me. Can you give me a bigger dress?
   → This dress is too small for me. Can you give me a bigger one?

2. We can't afford this apartment. Can you show us a cheaper apartment?
   → _____

3. A: These boys are very handsome! Which boys? B: Can you show me again?
   → _____

4. A: Which shoes are yours? B: The shoes by the window are mine.
   → _____

E Write the sentences again with *nobody*, *nothing*, or *nowhere*.

1. She isn't getting anywhere.
   → She is getting nowhere.

2. He didn't say anything about it.
   → _____

3. There isn't anything in the desk drawer.
   → _____

4. There wasn't anybody at home when I called. → _____

5. There was a thunderstorm during the night, but I didn't hear anything.
   → _____

A Look at the example and practice with a partner. Use the words below or invent your own. (Then change roles and practice again.)

1.

anything / Korea in Asia?
→ No / nothing

I.

Do you know anything about Korea in Asia?

No, I know nothing about that country.

2.

anything / Japan in Asia?
→ No / nothing

3.

anything / China in Asia?
→ No / nothing

4.

anything / India in Asia?
→ No / nothing

B Work with a partner. Which of the items below would you like to buy? Check(√) the appropriate boxes. Which one/ones do you like? Why? Which one/ones don't you like? Why not?

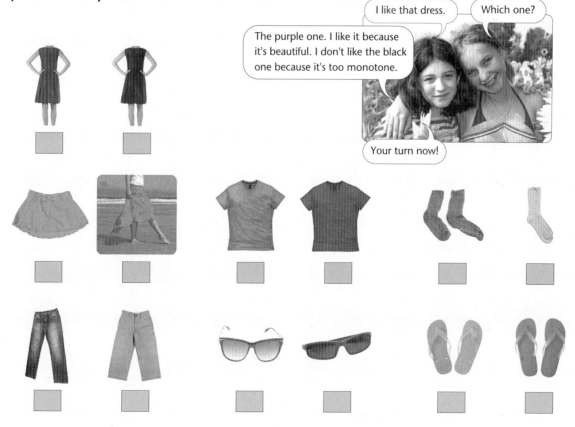

I like that dress.

Which one?

The purple one. I like it because it's beautiful. I don't like the black one because it's too monotone.

Your turn now!

The Passive

Learn & Practice 1

Passive: Affirmative (*Be + V-ed*)

- 우리가 흔히 만나는 거의 모든 문장은 주어가 동작의 주인이 되어 그 행위나 행동을 직접 하는 능동태(active voice) 문장 이에요. 하지만 수동태(passive voice)는 누가 어떤 동작을 했는가보다는 그 동작 자체를 중요하게 나타내거나 강조하기 위해서 사용해요. 따라서 목적어를 문장의 주어로 보내고 동사는 'be + v-ed(과거분사)'를 써요. 능동태에 있던 주어(행위 자)는 'by + 목적격(행위자)'으로 만들어 문장 뒤로 보냅니다. 수동태 문장은 '~가 …되가, …지다, …당하다, …를 받다' 등으로 해석이 돼요.

Active	Alexander Graham Bell **invented** the telephone. (Subject: Agent)
Passive	The telephone **was invented** by Alexander Graham Bell. (Agent: actor of the verb)

- 수동태 문장을 만드는 또 다른 이유는 어떤 동작이나 행위를 누가 했는지 잘 모르거나 중요하지 않은 경우, 그리고 말하지 않아도 명백히 누가 했는지를 알거나 보통 일반 사람들일 때 사용하고 행위자인 'by + 목적격'을 쓰지 않아요.

The temple **was destroyed** in 1999. (We don't know who destroyed it.)

English **is spoken** all over the world. (by people)

Rice **is grown** in Korea. (Who grows it isn't important.)

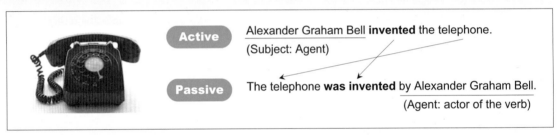

	Subject	Be	Verb + -ed	By	Object (Agent)
Present/Past Passive	I	am/was	invited	by	them. / her. / Tom.
	He/She/It / A Thing	is/was			
	You/We/They/Things	are/were			

A Write the past form and past participle form of the verbs given.

Base Form	Past	Be + Past Participle
1. speak	*spoke*	be *spoken*
2. write	_____	be _____
3. paint	_____	be _____
4. grow	_____	be _____

B Change the active verbs to passive verbs. Write the subject of the passive sentences.

1. Teenagers love movie stars. → _Movie stars are loved_ by teenagers.

2. The police caught the thief. → _____ by the police.

3. Jerry reads the magazine. → _____ by Jerry.

4. Andre Kim designed this dress. → _____ by Andre Kim.

5. Many people visit the museum. → _____ by many people.

Learn & Practice 2

Passive: *Negative* (*Be* + *Not* + V-*ed*)

- 수동태의 부정문은 be 동사 바로 뒤에 not을 붙여서 만들어요. be 동사의 부정문과 마찬가지로 문장에 be 동사가 있을 때에는 언제나 be 동사 뒤에 not을 써요.

The scary movie **wasn't seen** by many people.
→ Many people didn't see the scary movie.

This email **wasn't written** by Joshua.
→ Joshua didn't write this email.

Subject	Be	Not	Verb + -ed
I	am/was		
He/She/It / A Thing	is/was	not	invited
You/We/They/Things	are/were		

The cheese **wasn't eaten** by the mouse.
The bird **wasn't killed** by the cat.
I'm not invited to the party.

A Write the negative forms.

1. The window was broken by Susie. → _The window wasn't broken by Susie._

2. That film was made by Spielberg. → _____

3. Our mail is delivered by him. → _____

4. The office is cleaned every day. → _____

B Change these sentences from the active voice to the passive voice.

1. Kelly didn't invite me. → *I wasn't invited by Kelly.*

2. Many people don't visit the Seoul Tower. → _____

3. Mr. Brown doesn't teach the class. → _____

4. We didn't build these houses. → _____

5. She didn't make those cookies. → _____

Passive: Questions (*Be* + Subject + V-*ed*...?)

- 수동태를 의문문으로 만들 때에도 be 동사의 의문문과 똑같이 be 동사를 문장 맨 앞으로 보내고 물음표(?)를 써 주면 돼요.

- 대답은 be 동사 현재 또는 과거를 그대로 사용하여 yes나 no로 대답하고, 주어는 알맞은 대명사로 바꾸어 대답해요.

Q: **Is** the package **delivered** by him?
A: **Yes**, it **is**.

Q: **Were** they **found** in the library?
A: **No**, they **weren't**. They were found in the park.

Be	Subject	Verb + *-ed*	*By*	Object (Agent)
Am/Is/Are Was/Were	Subject(s)	**invented**	by	them? / him? / Peter?

A Change these sentences from the active voice to the passive voice.

1. Does Steve send the letters? → *Are the letters sent by Steve?*

2. Did they built the house? → _____

3. Did Emily mail the package? → _____

4. Does a cat catch a bird? → _____

5. Did you eat the apples? → _____

A First read the statements. Then write questions in the passive form and complete the short answers.

1. Q: Was the pizza delivered on time?

   A: Yes, _____it was_____. (The pizza was delivered on time.)

2. Q: _____

   A: Yes, _____. (Our mail is delivered by Mr. Smith.)

3. Q: _____

   Yes, _____. (Taxes are collected by the government.)

4. Q: _____

   A: No, _____. (Derek wasn't hired by that company.)

5. Q: _____

   A: Yes, _____. (Pasta was introduced to Europe by Marco Polo.)

6. Q: _____

   A: No, _____. (The classroom isn't cleaned by the students.)

B Change the following sentences from the passive voice to the active voice.

1.

Some cupcakes are baked by my neighbors.

My neighbors bake some cakes.

_____

2.

They are frightened by the movie.

_____

_____

3.

The coffee is served by the the waiter.

_____

_____

4.

A wheelchair is used by the patient.

_____

_____

5.

The hotel is designed by Eric.

_____

_____

6.

The plates are cleaned by Mrs. Wilson.

_____

_____

C Look at the pictures and answer the questions as in the example. Include the *by-*phrase only if necessary.

1.

A: What happened in this picture?

B: The mails were delivered by the postal carrier.

(the mails / deliver / the postal carrier)

2.

A: What happened in this picture?

B: _____

(someone / steal / my laptop)

3.

A: What happened in this picture?

B: _____

(My brother / clean / the room)

4.

A: What happened in this picture?

B: _____

(someone / build / that house / in the middle ages)

D Make sentences as in the example.

1.

Thomas Edison / invent /
the light bulb

→ Thomas Edison invented the light bulb. (Active)

→ The light bulb was invented by Thomas Edison. (Passive)

→ Was the light bulb invented by Thomas Edison? (Question)

2.

King Sejong / create
Hangeul / in the 15th century

→ _____ (Active)

→ _____ (Passive)

→ _____ (Question)

3.

A N
EXCELLENT
conceited Tragedie
O F

Shakespeare / write /
Romeo and Juliet

→ _____ (Active)

→ _____ (Passive)

→ _____ (Question)

A Look at the example and practice with a partner. Use the words below or invent your own. (Then change roles and practice again.)

1.

write / the *Harry Potter* books?
→ J. K. Rowling

1.

Who wrote the Harry Potter books?

They were written by J. K. Rowling.

2.

compose / this symphony?
→ Beethoven

3.

paint / *Sunflowers*
→ Vincent van Gogh

4.

build the Colosseum in Rome
→ 60,000 Jewish slaves

B Work with a partner. The following people are telling lies. Read what they say, then use the words in brackets to correct the false statements.

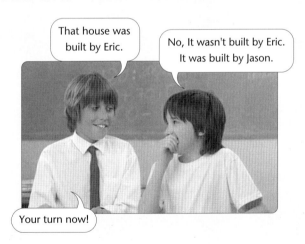

That house was built by Eric.

No, It wasn't built by Eric. It was built by Jason.

Your turn now!

1. Eric: I built that house.

   No → (Jason)

2. Sam: I found the lost puppy yesterday.

   No → (Ava)

3. Kevin: I drew the painting.

   No → (Jenny)

4. Nancy: I created Snoopy.

   No → (Charles M. Schulz)

5. Bob: I caught the thief last night.

   No → (the police)

6. Julie: I invented the potato chips.

   No → (George Crum)

Unit 10 Helping Verbs 1

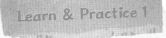
▶ Expressing Ability: *Can* and *Could*
▶ Using *Be Able To*
▶ Expressing Advice: *Should*, *Ought To*, *Had Better*
▶ Expressing Permission: *Can* and *May*

Learn & Practice 1

Expressing Ability: *Can* and *Could*

- 조동사 can은 현재나 미래의 능력을 나타내어 우리말로 '~할 수 있다'라는 뜻이 되고, could는 과거의 능력을 나타내어 '~할 수 있었다'라는 뜻이에요.
- 부정문은 조동사(can, could) 바로 뒤에 not을 붙이고 의문문은 조동사(can, could)를 문장 맨 앞으로 보내고 물음표를 써요. 대답은 yes/no로 하고 의문문에 사용한 조동사를 그대로 사용해서 답해요.

Monkeys **can** climb trees, but they **can't** fly.

Ability

We **could** ride a bicycle in the park yesterday.

Ⓐ Make *yes/no* questions and complete the short answers.

1. Jenna can drive a car.
Q: *Can Jenna drive a car?*　　　A: Yes, ___she can___.

2. Mark and Paul can play volleyball.
Q: _____　　　A: No, _____.

3. Steve can read and write.
Q: _____　　　A: Yes, _____.

4. She could solve the math problem.
Q: _____　　　A: No, _____.

5. I can speak Japanese.
Q: _____　　　A: No, _____.

Ⓑ Complete the sentences with *can*, *can't*, *could*, or *couldn't*.

1. Sarah is three years old. She ___can't___ write.

2. Peter is nineteen. He _____ drive a car.

3. Thompson is 70 years old. He _____ see very well, so he wears glasses.

4. When I was five years old, I _____ only count to ten.

5. It was cold yesterday, so we _____ go out.

Using *Be Able To*

- be able to는 조동사 can, could와 같은 의미인 '~할 수 있(었)다'라는 뜻으로 서로 바꾸어 쓸 수 있어요. 주어와 시제에 따라서 be 동사(am, is, are, was, were)만 고쳐 능력을 나타내는 표현을 만들 수 있어요.

Now	Past	Future

Jennifer **is able to** play the piano.	I **wasn't able to** hear them because of the noise.	We **will be able to** meet our grandparents tomorrow.

A Make sentences with the same meaning. Use *be able to*.

1. That girl can speak Korean. → *That girl is able to speak Korean.*

2. In the future we can go to the moon. → _____

3. She could play the piano. → _____

4. He can't run five miles. → _____

Expressing Advice: *Should, Ought To, Had Better*

- should와 ought to는 서로 같은 뜻으로 충고(advice) 또는 조언을 나타내며 '~하는 게 좋겠다'라는 뜻이에요. ought to 는 부정문과 의문문으로는 거의 쓰지 않아요.
- had better도 '~하는 게 좋겠다(낫겠다)'라는 충고나 조언의 뜻으로 비슷하지만 had better는 의미상 더 강한 어감이나 경고의 메시지(strong advice or warning)를 담고 있어요. 특히 had better는 어떤 특정한 상황에서 자주 쓰이고, 일반 적인 충고나 조언은 should나 ought to를 써요. 부정은 better 뒤에 not을 붙여요.

General	General	Specific

You **shouldn't** eat so much.	You **ought to** study English.	It's cold outside. You **had better** wear a coat.

- had better는 현재나 미래를 나타내는 표현이에요. had를 보고 과거 시제로 착각하면 안 돼요.

A Complete the sentences with *ought to* or *ought not to*.

1. It's your fault. You ___ought to___ apologize to her.

2. You _____ wear a seat belt in the car.

3. We _____ protect the environment.

4. You _____ pick flowers in the park.

B Complete the sentences with *had better* or *had better not*.

1. You ___had better not___ use your phone when you drive a car.

2. It's cold outside. You _____ wear a jacket.

3. Kelly got a bad cold. She _____ see a doctor.

4. Brian had a terrible headache. He _____ listen to loud music.

Learn & Practice 4

Expressing Permission: *Can* and *May*

- can과 may가 '~해도 좋다'라는 뜻으로 허락(give permission)을 나타낼 때 서로 같은 역할을 해요. 다만 may가 can 보다 좀 더 공손한 표현이에요. can과 may 뒤에 not을 붙인 부정문은 '~해서는 안 된다'라는 허락의 부정(refuse permission)을 나타내요.

- 상대방에게 정중하게 부탁이나 허락을 요구할 때 May I...? 또는 Could/Can I...?를 써요. May I...?가 가장 정중한 표현 이고 일상에서는 Could I...?를 가장 많이 쓰고 친구나 가족과 같이 편안한 사이에서는 Can I...?를 주로 써요.

You **can** sit next to me.

You **may** not camp here. It's dangerous.

May (Could/Can) I use your smartphone?

A Complete the sentences with *can, may, can I,* or *may I*.

1. A: You ___can___ use my computer.   B: Thanks. (They know each other.)

2. A: _____ turn on the television?   B: Certainly. (They know each other.)

3. A: _____ have another napkin?   B: Sure. (They don't know each other.)

4. You _____ use my dictionary. (They don't know each other.)

5. A: _____ speak to him?   B: Just a minute. I'll get him. (They don't know each other.)

A Read the situations. Make questions with *may I* or *can I* as in the example.

1. Your phone is out of order. You want to use your neighbor's telephone.

   → *May I use your telephone?*_____

2. You want to invite some friends to lunch. What do you say to your mother?

   → _____

3. You ask your father for permission to watch TV with your sister, Alexa.

   → _____

4. You have a stomachache. You ask your teacher to go to the toilet.

   → _____

5. You are in a department store. You see some dresses you like, and you want to try them on. You say to the salesperson.

   → _____

B Complete the sentences with *should* and *shouldn't* and the verbs in brackets.

1. If you need a pencil, you ____*shouldn't say*____, "Give me that pencil."; you ____*should say*____, "May I borrow your pencil, please?" (say / say)

2. If someone doesn't speak your language very well, you _____ fast; you _____ slowly and carefully. (speak / speak)

3. If people want to live until they're very old, they _____ a lot of fruit and vegetables; they _____ a lot of junk food. (eat / eat)

4. In a library, you _____ careful with your money; you _____ your bag on a chair in a library. (be / leave)

5. When people are traveling by plane, they _____ comfortable clothes; they _____ their mobile phones. (wear / use)

C Rewrite the sentences using the words given.

1. It is a good idea to tell your friend the truth.
   → *You had better tell your friend the truth.*

   had better

2. Jessica has been ill for three days. Why doesn't she see a doctor?
   → _____

   ought to

3. It is a good idea to leave now.
   → _____

   had better

4. How about buying Haley a smartphone for her birthday?
   → _____

   ought to

D Write five things you couldn't do before, but you can do now.

1. *Five years ago, I couldn't swim, but I can swim well now.*

2. _____

3. _____

4. _____

5. _____

6. _____

E Rewrite the sentences using the correct form of *be able to* in place of *can/could* + verb.

1. She can walk for 10 hours.
   → *She is able to walk for 10 hours.*

2. They could ride a bicycle in the park.
   → _____

3. Can you write a letter to your mother?
   → _____

4. I tried very hard, but I couldn't do all of my math problems.
   → _____

5. We can't see him until next week.
   → _____

A Look at the example and practice with a partner. Use the words below or invent your own. (Then change roles and practice again.)

I.

 When I was a child, I could do a handstand. Could you do a handstand?

 No, I couldn't. I could play the piano.

1. do a handstand
→ No / play the piano

2. use a computer
→ No / play a musical instrument

3. write with my left hand
→ No / catch a small bird

4. read English
→ No / eat with chopsticks

5. make an omelet
→ No / make popcorn

6. make a big snowman
→ No / see a ghost at night

B Read the situations and give strong advice. Using *had better* or *had better not* and your own words.

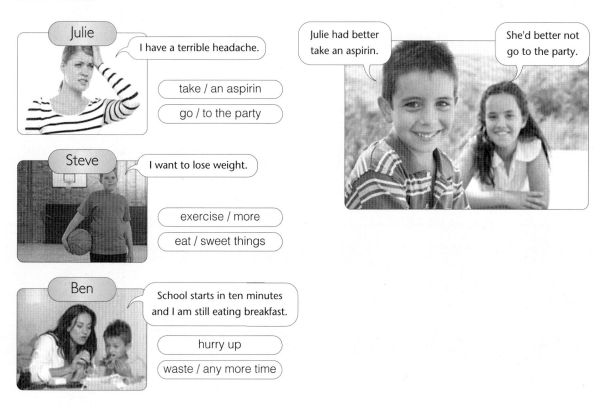

Julie

I have a terrible headache.

take / an aspirin

go / to the party

Julie had better take an aspirin.

She'd better not go to the party.

Steve

I want to lose weight.

exercise / more

eat / sweet things

Ben

School starts in ten minutes and I am still eating breakfast.

hurry up

waste / any more time

Unit **11** **Helping Verbs 2**

Unit Focus

▶ *Must*, *Have To*, and *Have Got To* to Express Obligation and Necessit*
▶ *Not Have To* and *Must Not* to Express Lack of Necessity and Prohibit*
▶ *May*, *Might*, and *Could* to Express Possibility
▶ Making Logical Conclusions: *Must*

Learn & Practice 1

Must, Have To, and *Have Got To* to Express Obligation and Necessity

- must, have to, have got to는 '~해야 한다'라는 필요와 의무(necessity and obligation)를 나타내요. 특히, must는 상대방에게 중요성을 강조하여 선택의 여지가 없는 강한 의무나 필요를 나타내요.

- have got to는 글을 쓸 때(in writing)보다는 말할 때(in speaking) 주로 써요. 주어가 3인칭 단수일 때에는 has (got) to를 써야 해요.

- must와 have got to는 과거형이 없고, 거의 의문문으로 만들지 않아요. 과거형으로는 had to를 쓰고, 의문문을 만들 때에는 'Do/Does/Did + 주어 + have to…?'로 만들어요.

| Amy **must** return the book to the library. | Q: **Did** you **have to** go to the bank? A: Yes, I did. | I've **got to** see the dentist tomorrow. |

	Statement	**Question**
Present or Future	I **must** study now/tonight. They **have (got) to** study now/tonight.	Q: **Does** she **have to** work? A: **Yes**, she **does**. / **No**, she **doesn't**. Q: **Do** I **have to** work? A: **Yes**, you **do**. / **No**, you **don't**.
Past	We **had to** study yesterday.	**Did** they **have to** study yesterday? - **Yes**, they **did**. / **No**, they **didn't**.

Ⓐ Rewrite the sentences with the words in brackets.

1. She must study for the test.

   → (have to) *She has to study for the test.*

   → (have got to) *She has got to study for the test.*

2. They must be quiet.

   → (have to) _____

   → (have got to) _____

3. You must get her to a doctor.

   → (have to) _____

   → (have got to) _____

B Make *yes/no* questions and complete the short answers.

1. She had to go to the dentist. Q: *Did she have to go to the dentist?* A: No, *she didn't* .

2. She has to turn off the TV. Q: _____ A: Yes, _____ .

3. We have to get up early. Q: _____ A: No, _____ .

4. He had to stay at home. Q: _____ A: Yes, _____ .

Learn & Practice 2

Not Have To and *Must Not* to Express Lack of Necessity and Prohibition

- have to와 must는 긍정문에서 '~해야 한다'라는 같은 뜻으로 쓰이지만 뜻이 같지만 부정문에서는 전혀 다른 뜻이 되므로 주의해야 해요. must not(=mustn't)은 '~해서는 안 된다'라는 뜻으로서 강한 금지를 나타내는 반면, have to의 부정인 don't/doesn't/didn't have to는 '~할 필요가 없(었)다'라는 뜻으로 불필요함을 나타내기 때문에 어떤 일에 대해 다른 선택의 여지가 있을 때 사용해요. '~해서는 안 된다(must not)'라고 해석하면 안 돼요.

You **mustn't** talk during the exam.

Tomorrow is a holiday.
Ron **doesn't have to** go to class.

Yesterday was a holiday.
Ron **didn't have to** go to class.

A Complete the sentences with *mustn't* or *don't/didn't have to*.

1. A: You _____*mustn't*_____ do that again! It was very naughty!
   B: I'm sorry.

2. A: You _____ be late tonight.
   B: I won't. I'll be home early.

3. A: You _____ buy a gift for Allison's birthday.
   B: Alright. I'll just send a card.

4. A: Yesterday was Saturday.
   B: We _____ go to school.

5. A: You _____ forget to pay the bills today.
   B: I've already done it.

May, Might, and *Could* to Express Possibility

- 현재나 미래에 어떤 일이 일어날 가능성에 대한 확신이 없을 때(50% 이하)에는 may, might, could를 써서 '~일지 모른다'라는 뜻의 가능성을 나타내요. 그런데 가능성을 나타내는 might와 could를 과거로 생각하면 안돼요. 현재나 미래를 나타내는 표현이에요.

- 부정문은 may와 might 바로 뒤에 not을 붙이고 may not과 might not의 축약형을 쓰지 않아요. 가능성을 나타낼 때에 could는 부정문으로 쓰지 않아요.

A: Where are you going for vacation?
B: I'm not sure. I **may/might/could** go to Italy.

Jada **may/might not** go out tonight.
She isn't feeling well.

Ⓐ Read the underlined words and write *possibility*, *ability*, or *permission*.

1. I may not go to school tomorrow. → *possibility*

2. That might not be true. → _____

3. She could drive a stick-shift car. → _____

Making Logical Conclusions: *Must*

- 현재 상황에 대한 논리적 이유가 있는 강한 확신(95%)을 나타낼 때 must (be)를 쓰고 '~임에 틀림없다'라고 해석해요. can't는 '~일 리가 없다'라는 의미로 거의 100%에 가까운 확신을 나타낼 때 써요. 현재의 사실로 100% 확정할 때에는 조동사 없는 현재형을 써요.

A: Do you know where Chloe is?
B: She **is** at home now. (100% certainty)
   She is eating something. She **must** be hungry. (95% certainty)
A: She had lunch half an hour ago. She **can't** be hungry. (almost 100% sure)

Ⓐ Complete the sentences with *must* or *can't*, as in the example.

1. Tom plays soccer every day. He ____*must*____ like to play soccer.

2. Karen is yawning. She _____ be sleepy.

3. Kate ate dinner ten minutes ago. Don't set a place for her. She _____ be hungry.

A Write sentences with *may* or *may not*.

1. It's possible that I'll go to the movies. → I may go to the movies.

2. It's possible that it will rain today. → _____

3. It's possible that Cindy won't change her job. → _____

4. It's possible that Sarah will go to Korea next week. → _____

5. It's possible that I won't have time to go out tonight. → _____

B What about you? What are you going to do this weekend? Use *might (not)* in your answers.

1. I might play badminton with my father. 2. _____

3. _____ 4. _____

C Look at the pictures and prompts. Ask and answer questions, as in the example.

1.

he / go to the supermarket yesterday
→ buy some meat

Q: Why did he go to the supermarket
yesterday?
A: Because he had to buy some meat.

2.

she / go to the post office yesterday
→ post some letters

Q: _____
_____
A: _____

3.

they / call the babysitter yesterday
→ attend a meeting

Q: _____
_____
A: _____

4.

she / go to the hospital yesterday
→ visit a friend

Q: _____
_____
A: _____

D Complete the sentences with *must* or *must not*. Use the words in brackets.

1.
(tired today)

Mary worked ten hours today.

→ She *must be tired today* _____.

2.
(work on Friday)

Lisa plays golf all day on Fridays.

→ She _____.

3.
(have a pet)

There is a bowl of food on the kitchen floor.

→ Olivia _____.

E Tell if you have to or don't have to do the following. For affirmative statements, you can also use *have got to*.

1. speak English in class → *I have got to speak English in class. OR I don't have*
   to speak English in class.

2. use a dictionary to read the newspaper → _____

3. come to school every day → _____

4. use public transportation → _____

5. talk to the teacher after class → _____

6. memorize vocabularies → _____

F Look at the pictures. Make sentences with *must* or *mustn't*. Use the words in brackets.

1.
run in the hallway

→ *You mustn't run in the hallway.* _____

2.
listen to the teacher

→ _____

3.
talk with your friend

→ _____

4.
sleep in class

→ _____

A Look at the example and practice with a partner. Use the words below or invent your own. (Then change roles and practice again.)

I.

 What do you have to do tomorrow?

 I have to go to the grocery store to buy some fruit.

1. go to the grocery store
   → buy some fruit

2. go to the supermarket
   → get some milk

3. go downtown
   → go to the family restaurant

4. go to the library
   → borrow the library books

5. stay home
   → watch a movie on TV

6. go to the movie theater
   → buy the tickets to see the movie

B Work with a partner. Two people are having lunch in a restaurant. Some of their belongings are on their tables. Make a logical deduction about the owners.

Look at the first table. There is a handbag on the table.

The owner must be a woman.

Your turn now!

Unit 12 Present Perfect 1

Unit Focus

▶ Present Perfect: Meaning
▶ Present Perfect: Forms
▶ Present Perfect: Negative Statements and Questions

Learn & Practice 1

Present Perfect: Meaning

- 현재완료(have/has + v-ed)는 '과거에 시작했는데'와 '지금은 ~하다'라는 의미를 둘 다 포함하고 있는 시제예요. '현재까지 ~했다'라는 현재의 의미가 포함되어 있어 과거의 특정한 시간을 언급하지 않아요. 정확한 시간을 나타내지 않는 것은 정확한 시간이 중요하지 않고 행위나 상태에 더 초점을 두고 있기 때문이랍니다. 특정한 과거의 시간을 나타내려면 과거 시제를 써야 해요.

Tom and Ava **have bought** a new sports car.

Jessica **has broken** her right leg.

- 현재완료는 과거에 시작한 동작이나 상태가 현재까지 계속 지속되고 있을 때 사용해요. 주로 for나 since와 함께 자주 쓰여요.

I **have worked** in this company *for* five years.

Kathy **has studied** Korean *since* 2011.

- 현재완료는 조금 전에 막 끝난 동작을 나타낼 때에도 쓸 수 있어요. 현재 눈에 보이는 결과를 토대로 나타내는 거예요.

She **has painted** the house.
(The house was white. Now it is sky-blue.)

They **have arrived** at the airport.

A Write *a, b, c,* or *d* in the blank to show the meaning of the present perfect in each sentence.

> a. past action continuing up to present   b. repeated past action
> c. past action without specific time   d. completed action

1. ___a___ Have you had this backache for a long time?

2. _____ I have lived in France.

3. _____ How many colds have you had this year?

4. _____ She's been sick since August.

5. _____ I have already finished my homework.

Learn & Practice 2

Present Perfect: Forms

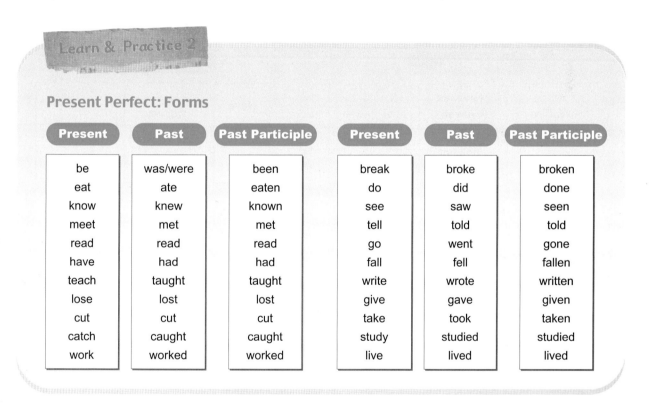

Present	Past	Past Participle	Present	Past	Past Participle
be	was/were	been	break	broke	broken
eat	ate	eaten	do	did	done
know	knew	known	see	saw	seen
meet	met	met	tell	told	told
read	read	read	go	went	gone
have	had	had	fall	fell	fallen
teach	taught	taught	write	wrote	written
lose	lost	lost	give	gave	given
cut	cut	cut	take	took	taken
catch	caught	caught	study	studied	studied
work	worked	worked	live	lived	lived

A Circle the correct words.

1. Lisa has (saw / (seen)) this movie twice so far.

2. Jamie (have / has) seen the rainbow.

3. I have (spoke / spoken) to him about it many times.

4. We (have / has) visited Seoul several times.

5. They have (ate / eaten) Vietnamese food.

6. Bill has (broke / broken) his right arm, so he can't do his project.

Present Perfect: Negative Statements and Questions

- 현재완료의 부정문은 have/has 뒤에 not을 붙여 만들어요.
- 의문문은 have/has를 문장 맨 앞으로 보내고 문장 뒤에 물음표(?)를 붙이면 돼요. 대답은 yes/no로 하고 의문문에 사용한 have/has를 그대로 사용해서 답해요.

We **haven't finished** breakfast yet.

Q: **Have** you **lived** here for a long time?
A: **No**, I **haven't**.

Negative		
I/You We/They	have not (= haven't)	studied Japanese.
He/She/It	has not (= hasn't)	

Question		
Have	I/you we/they	worked here long?
Has	he/she/it	

Q: **Has** she **lost** her key?   A: **Yes**, she **has**.
Q: **Have** you **seen** a movie star before?   A: **No**, I **haven't**.
Q: **Has** it **snowed** for 5 days?   A: **Yes**, it **has**.

A Use the prompts to make sentences with the present perfect.

1. I / not feel / well all week   →   *I haven't felt well all week.*

2. We / not see / the movie   →   _____

3. Eric / clean / the house / ?   →   _____

4. Linda / be / to Thailand / ?   →   _____

5. I / not leave my phone / in the subway   →   _____

6. We / not prepare / for the party   →   _____

7. She / ride / a horse / ?   →   _____

A Look at the pictures and make sentences. Use the present perfect simple.

1.

He / win / the gold medal

→ He has won the gold medal.

2.

Tom / break / his leg

→ _____

3.

I / work / very hard for this exam

→ _____

4.

They / be married / for 40 years

→ _____

B Read the situations, then write appropriate sentences using the verbs given.

1. I'm looking for my smartphone. I can't find it. (lose)

   → I have lost my smartphone.

2. Kathy's hair was dirty. Now it is clean. (wash)

   → _____

3. Scott weighed 70 kilograms. Now he weighs 60. (lose weight)

   → _____

4. The car has just stopped because there isn't any more gas in the tank. (run out of gas)

   → _____

5. Yesterday Kevin was playing soccer. Now he can't walk because his leg is in a cast. (break)

   → _____

6. Ava went to China. She is in China. (go)

   → _____

C Look at the pictures and write questions and answers. Use the present perfect tense.

1.

they / take / yoga lessons?
→ No / Taekwondo lessons

Q: Have they taken yoga lessons?

A: No, they haven't. They have taken

   Taekwondo lessons.

2.

Scarlett / meet / a famous cyclist
→ No / a famous guitarist

Q: _____

A: _____

   _____

3.

Daniel / try / water skiing?
→ No / windsurfing

Q: _____

A: _____

   _____

4.

Richard and Nancy / read / a magazine?
→ No / a newspaper

Q: _____

A: _____

   _____

D Write negative sentences in present perfect simple.

The weather was wonderful today. So the children were in the park all afternoon and have not done their household chores:

1. Sarah / not / wash the dishes   →   Sarah hasn't washed the dishes.

2. Tara / not / clean the kitchen   →   _____

3. Jenny and Peter / not / water the plants   →   _____

4. Jack and Sally / not / do their homework   →   _____

5. Alex / not / feed the hamster   →   _____

6. Tony and Ben / not / tidy up their rooms   →   _____

A Look at the example and practice with a partner. Use the words below or invent your own. (Then change roles and practice again.)

I.
she / visit / the museum?
→ Yes

I.
 Has she visited the museum?

 Yes, she has visited the museum.

2.
she / work / at the bank?
→ Yes

3.
Martin / buy / the bicycle?
→ Yes

4.
they / travel / by airplane?
→ No

5.
Christina / eat / Kimchi before?
→ No

6.
Sarah / read / a magazine
→ No

B Work with a partner. Ask and answer questions using the phrases given.

eat Korean food

ride a horse

ride a speed boat

write an email to your teacher

do your homework

try windsurfing

take violin lessons

see the Mayan Temples

play golf

Have you eaten Korean food?

No, I haven't eaten Korean food.

Your turn now!

Learn & Practice 1

Present Perfect: *For* and *Since*

- 현재완료의 계속은 '과거에 시작한 일을 현재까지 쭉 ~해 왔다'라는 뜻으로 for나 since와 함께 자주 쓰여요.
- for는 '~ 동안에'란 뜻으로 시간의 길이(a length of time)를 나타내고, since는 '~ 이래로'란 뜻으로 과거에 그 일이 시작된 특정 시점(the start of the period)을 나타내요.
- How long...?으로 묻는 현재완료 시제의 질문은 과거에 시작해서 지금까지의 어떤 행동이나 상태의 특정한 기간을 물어보기 때문에 for와 since를 이용하여 대답해야 해요.

I met Lisa at the university three years ago. Now it is 2014.
Q: *How long* **have** you **known** Lisa?
A: I **have known** her **for** three years.
   I **have known** her **since** 2011.

	For		Since
for	three days four months five weeks two days three hours twenty minutes a minute a long time	**since**	2012 last year (last) October (last) Thursday yesterday this morning 9 o'clock this morning

Ⓐ Complete the sentences with the present perfect of the verbs in brackets and write *for* or *since*.

1. Jack ___*has been*___ (be) the manager ___*since*___ 1996.

2. We _____ (not / see) her _____ last year.

3. She _____ (be) a teacher _____ 10 years.

4. I _____ (know) her sister _____ September.

5. My sister _____ (work) at the hospital _____ 5 years.

6. He _____ (teach) English _____ twenty years.

Present Perfect: *Ever* and *Never*

- ever는 현재완료 시제와 함께 써서 '(지금까지) ~해 본 적 있니?'라고 물어볼 때 의문문에서 사용해요. ever의 위치는 주어와 과거분사(past participle) 사이에 써요.
- never는 부정의 의미로 현재완료 시제와 함께 쓰면 '(지금까지) 한 번도 ~ 해 본 적이 없다'라는 뜻이 돼요. never의 위치는 have/has 바로 뒤에 써요.

Q: I have **never** seen the Colosseum. Have you **ever** seen it?
A: Yes, I have. I have been there many times.

Have/Has	Subject	Ever	Past Participle	
Have	you	**ever**	been	to Rome?

Subject	Have/Has	Never	Past Participle	
He	has	**never**	played	soccer.

A Make sentences as in the example.

1. He / have / never / a girlfriend → He has never had a girlfriend.
2. I / ride / never / a bicycle → _____
3. you / climb / ever / a mountain / ? → _____
4. Kate / swim / ever / in a river / ? → _____

Have Gone (To) vs. *Have Been (To)*

- have/has gone (to)는 '~에(로) 가버렸다(그래서 지금 여기 없다)'라는 뜻이고 have/has been (to)는 '~에 갔다 왔다, ~에 가 본 적이 있다'라는 뜻이에요.

Q: Hello, Mrs. Brown! Is Peter at home now?
A: He isn't here. He **has gone** to the department store.

Q: Where **have** you **been**, Sam?
A: I **have been** to the department store.

Ⓐ **Look at the pictures and complete the sentences with** *have/has* **been or** *have/has* **gone.**

1.
My friends aren't here.
They ___have gone___ to
Spain with their parents.

2.
They aren't at home.
They _____ to
the shops.

3.
My dad _____
to the shops. He has
gifts for everyone.

Present Perfect: *Already, Yet,* **and** *Just*

- already는 '이미'라는 뜻으로 이미 끝난 일 또는 기대했던 것보다 일찍 완료된 일을 강조하기 위해서 사용해요. already 는 have/has 바로 뒤에 써요.
- just는 '방금 전에, 막'이라는 뜻으로 방금 전 또는 조금 전에 끝난 일을 나타내요. just의 위치는 have/has 바로 뒤에 써 요.
- yet은 부정문에서 '아직'이란 뜻으로 기대(생각)하고 있던 일이나 행위가 끝나지 않았을 때 사용해요. yet은 문장 맨 끝에 써요. yet이 의문문에 쓰였을 경우 '벌써'라는 뜻으로 기대(생각)하고 있던 일이 벌써 끝난 상황으로 약간의 놀람을 나타내 요.

Jenny has **just** been to the library.
She has **already** eaten dinner with her friends.

Q: Has she returned the library books **yet**?
A: No, she hasn't returned them **yet**.

Ⓐ **Add the word in brackets to each sentence.**

1. I've read an interesting book. (just) → *I've just read an interesting book.*

2. Tom has finished his work. (just) → _____

3. They have eaten their lunch. (already) → _____

4. My brother hasn't done his homework. (yet) → _____

5. Has the plane arrived? (yet) → _____

6. They have bought souvenirs. (already) → _____

A Complete the sentences as in the example. Use the present perfect of the verbs in brackets.

1.

A: How long have you been in Korea _____ ?

B: I have been in Korea since 2006.

A: ___Have___ you ___made___ (made) any friends?

B: Yes, I ___have made___ a lot of friends, but my Korean hasn't improved.

2.

A: _____ ?

B: I have studied English for seven years, but I _____ (not speak) for a long time.

A: Neither have I. I haven't spoken English with foreigners, but I _____ (watch) English movies for many years.

B Ask and answer questions as in the example.

1. Sue / live here / three years

Q: How long has Sue lived here? _____

A: She has lived here for three years. _____

2. Brad / be / a teacher / 2008

Q: _____

A: _____

3. They / work / here / six months

Q: _____

A: _____

4. Nicole / know / them / last year

Q: _____

A: _____

5. Sarah / be / ill / Saturday

Q: _____

A: _____

C It's 9 o'clock in the morning. Look at the box and write what Sarah has (not) done. Use the present perfect verbs with *already*, *yet*, and *just*.

1. She has just drunken a glass of milk.

2. She hasn't got dressed yet.

3. She has already done her homework.

4. _____

5. _____

6. _____

7. _____

8. _____

1. drink a glass of milk	8:55 (O)
2. get dressed	(X)
3. do her homework	(O)
4. write letters	(X)
5. call her father	8:57 (O)
6. clean her bedroom	(O)
7. make sandwiches	(X)
8. brush her teeth	8:59 (O)

D Look at the pictures. Use the prompts to write questions and answers, as in the example. Use the information.

1.
be / to Australia?
→ No / Brazil

Q: Have you ever been to Australia?
A: No, I've never been to Australia, but
   I've been to Brazil.

2.
play / baseball?
→ No / volleyball

Q: _____
A: _____
   _____

3.
work / in a restaurant?
→ No / in a library

Q: _____
A: _____
   _____

4.
see / the Eiffel Tower in Paris?
→ No / the Taj Mahal in India

Q: _____
A: _____
   _____

A Look at the example and practice with a partner. Use the words below or invent your own. (Then change roles and practice again.)

1.

you / yet / study for the geography exam / ?
→ Yes / already

1.

Have you studied for the geography exam yet?

Yes, I have. I've already studied for the geography exam.

2.

Kristen / yet / eat / lunch / ?
→ Yes / already

3.

Lauren / yet / buy / the dress / ?
→ Yes / just

4.

they / yet / get married / ?
→ just

B Work with a partner. Ask questions beginning with *Have you ever...?* and give answers.

Have you ever been to Hollywood?

Yes, I've been to Hollywood. or No, I haven't. I've never been to Hollywood.

Your turn to ask!

1. be to Hollywood

2. play the guitar

3. fly in a helicopter

4. eat Thai food

5. swim in a river

6. be to China

7. ride an elephant

8. give your teacher a gift

9. eat raw fish

10. see the skeleton of a dinosaur

11. try bungee jumping

12. make a birthday cake

13. hear strange noises at night

Unit 14 Present Perfect 3

**Unit Focus**
- ▶ Present Perfect vs. Simple Past: Forms
- ▶ Present Perfect vs. Simple Past: Meaning
- ▶ Using *Since*

Learn & Practice 1

Present Perfect vs. Simple Past: Forms

- 과거 시제를 만들 때에는 주로 동사에 -d 또는 -ed를 붙여서 만들고 be 동사의 과거는 was와 were를 써요.
- 현재완료 시제는 동사를 'have + v-ed'로 만드는데 v-ed는 과거 시제를 만드는 방법과 같아요. 즉, 과거 시제 앞에 have/has를 붙이면 현재완료 시제가 되는 거예요.

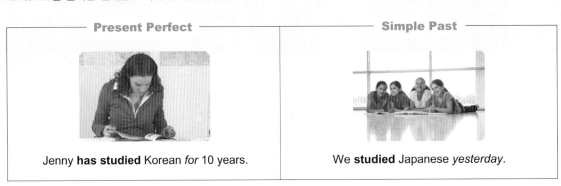

Present Perfect	Simple Past
Jenny **has studied** Korean *for* 10 years.	We **studied** Japanese *yesterday*.

Time Expressions	**Time Expressions**
ever, before, never, just, how long, since, for, already, yet, so far, before	ago, yesterday, in 1999 last night/week/month/year, etc.

A Complete the sentences with the words in parentheses. Use the present perfect or the simple past.

1. A: I ____saw____ (see) Jennifer yesterday.

   B: Oh really? I ___have not seen___ (not / see) her for a long time.

2. A: What _____ you _____ (do) last Saturday?

   B: I _____ (stay) at home.

3. A: _____ you _____ (finish) your homework yet?

   B: Yes, I _____ (finish) it two hours ago.

4. A: _____ you _____ (be) to Turkey?

   B: Yes, I _____ (go) there last summer.

Present Perfect vs. Simple Past: Meaning

- 현재완료 시제는 가까운 불특정한 과거에 막 끝난 동작이나 현재까지 지속되고 있는 동작이나 상태를 나타내요. 즉, 행위 자체에 초점을 맞추고 있어 과거의 어느 때인지를 나타내는 구체적인 시점이 중요하지 않아요.
- 과거 시제는 과거에 시작한 일이 과거에 끝났으며 현재와는 전혀 무관한 과거의 사실만을 나타내요. 따라서 yesterday와 같이 과거의 구체적인 시점을 언급하면 과거 시제를 써야 해요.

Simple Past	Present Perfect
• 과거의 정확한 시점이 언급된 동작이나 상태	• 과거의 동작을 나타내지만 과거의 특정한 시점을 알 수 없거나 언급되지 않은 동작

They saw the movie *yesterday*.
(When? Yesterday. The specific time is mentioned.)

Have you ever seen the movie?
(When? We don't know. The specific time isn't mentioned.)

- 과거에 시작하여 과거에 끝난 동작이나 상태

- 과거에 시작하여 현재까지 지속되고 있는 동작이나 상태

Kathy **was** a fashion model for 10 years.
(She's not a fashion model anymore.)

Ava **has been** a cheerleader for 5 years.
(She started working as a cheerleader 5 years ago and she still is.)

A Put the words in brackets into the present perfect or the simple past tense.

1. She ___*didn't go*___ (not / go) to school yesterday because she was ill.

2. _____ (you / ever / fly) a kite?

3. He _____ (go) to the movie theater last week.

4. _____ (you / eat) all the chocolate cake last night?

5. Mike _____ (visit) five European countries so far.

B Use the prompts to make sentences with the present perfect or the simple past.

1. she / be / sick / since August → *She has been sick since August.*

2. we / buy / a new car / last week → _____

3. Diane and Paul / arrive / yet / ? → _____

4. you / ever / be / to Florida / ? → _____

5. Kelly and I / be / good friends / since 2005 → _____

6. he / forget / to turn off the TV / yesterday → _____

Learn & Practice 3

Using *Since*

- 현재완료 계속은 '과거부터 쭉 ~해 왔다'라는 뜻으로 현재완료 시제 형태인 'have + v-ed'는 for나 since와 함께 자주 써요. since는 뒤에 '주어 + 동사'가 함께 올 수 있는데 이때 동사는 반드시 '과거' 시제를 써야 해요. '~ 이래로 지금까지'라고 해석해요.

- 과거의 구체적인 한 시점을 나타내는 when은 현재완료와 함께 쓰지 못해요. when 뒤에 '주어 + 동사'가 함께 오는데 이때에도 동사는 과거 시제를 써야 해요.

Jenny **has worked** here since she **finished** university.

Lily **was** happy when she **passed** the exam.

Subject	Past Participle	*Since*	Subject	Simple Past
Tom	**has studied** English	since	he	**was** a student.

Subject	Simple Past	*When*	Subject	Simple Past
Tom	**studied** English	when	he	**was** a student.

A Complete the sentences with *since* or *when*.

1. I liked to paint ___*when*___ I was alone.

2. Susan hasn't visited us _____ she got married.

3. The actors walked offstage _____ the play finished.

4. We have been together _____ we first saw each other.

A Read the information and write sentences with the present perfect and the simple past. Use *for* and *since*.

1.
Alice

I live in Korea now. I started to live in Japan in 2005. I came to Korea in 2008.

2.
Cindy

I live in Turkey now. I started to live in Singapore in 2008. I came to Turkey in 2012.

3.
Wilson

I live in England now. I started to live in Canada in 1999. I came to England in 2009.

1. Alice lived in Japan for three years.   2. Alice has lived in Korea since 2008.

3. _____   4. _____

5. _____   6. _____

B Write questions using the prompts. Use the present perfect or the simple past. Read the answers before you write the questions.

1. how long / Olivia / live / in France?
   Q: How long has Olivia lived in France? _____   A: Since 2007.

2. when / Bob / lose / his job?
   Q: _____   A: two weeks ago.

3. what time / you / wash / your car?
   Q: _____   A: At 10:00 a.m.

4. how long / Kimberly / have / her driving licence?
   Q: _____   A: Since January.

5. when / Christina / go out?
   Q: _____   A: Ten minutes ago.

6. how long / your father / be / in hospital?
   Q: _____   A: Since last week.

C Look at the list of exciting things Eric wants to do and write sentences. Use the present perfect or the simple past as in the examples.

Exciting Things To Do
• ride a horse (✓) - yesterday
• try bungee jumping (x) - yet
• try scuba diving (✓) - already
• travel around Australia (x)- yet
• taste a snake (✓) - two days ago
• stay in the jungle for a week (✓) - already
• try canoeing (✓) - already
• visit Egypt (x) - yet

1. Eric rode a horse yesterday   2. Eric hasn't tried bungee jumping yet.

3. _____ 4. _____

5. _____ 6. _____

7. _____ 8. _____

D Look at the prompts and write sentences as in the example. Use the present perfect + *since* + the simple past.

1. Jenny / lose / ten kilos   she / start / going / to the gym

→ Jenny has lost ten kilos since she started going to the gym.

2. Kelly / improve / her Spanish   she / decide / to study more

→ _____

3. Sarah / not go out / with her friends   she / find / a new job

→ _____

4. my wife and I / know / each other   we / are / in elementary school

→ _____

5. I / meet / Alexis   I / am / a freshman / in high school

→ _____

A Look at the example and practice with a partner. Use the words below or invent your own. (Then change roles and practice again.)

I.

Jose / ever / try / waterskiing?
→ Yes / last week

I.

Has Jose ever tried waterskiing?

Yes, he has. He tried waterskiing last week.

2.

you / ever / eat / sushi / before?
→ Yes / yesterday

3.

Vivian / ever / rent / a car?
→ Yes / two years ago

4.

you / ever / see / a shooting star?
→ Yes / 10 years ago

B Work with a partner. Look at the table below. Ask and answer questions as in the example.

Has Henry bought T-shirts?

Yes, he has already bought them. He bought them yesterday.

Your turn to ask!

Henry	buy / T-shirts	O	already / yesterday
Sarah	turn off the gas	X	yet
Lisa	eat raw fish / before	X	yet
Jennifer	see / a ghost	O	already / last night
Ava	ever / catch / a fish	O	already / last month
Steve and Jessica	eat Italian food	X	yet
William	play a video game	O	already / on Friday

Comparison 1

▶ *The Same (As)*, *Similar (To)*, and *Different (From)*
▶ Comparatives
▶ *As...As* and *Not As...As*

The Same (As), *Similar (To)*, and *Different (From)*

- 두 가지 대상을 서로 비교하여 '~와 똑같다'는 the same (as), '~와 비슷하다'는 similar (to), '~와는 다르다'는 different (from)을 써요. same은 형용사지만 정관사 *the*를 써요.

- 세 가지 모두 형용사로 사용되기 때문에 be 동사 뒤에 단독으로 쓰거나, 비교 대상을 뒤에 쓸 경우에는 the same은 as, similar는 to, different는 from 뒤에 비교 대상을 두어요.

- 'the same + 명사 + as'의 형태로 the same과 as 사이에 명사를 자주 써요. 반대말인 'not the same + 명사 + as'는 형용사와 부사를 이용한 비교급으로 나타낼 수 있어요.

Photo A　　　Photo B	Photo A　　　Photo B	Photo A　　　Photo B
Photos A and B are **the same**. A is **the same as** B. A is **the same** color **as** B.	Photos A and B are **similar**. A is **similar to** B.	Photos A and B are **different**. A is **different from** B.

He's **not the same age as** his wife.
→ His wife is **younger**.

A　　　　　B

Wrestler B is **not the same weight as** wrestler A.
Wrestler A is **fatter**.

Ⓐ **Underline the correct form.**

1. My bicycle is (the same / <u>the same as</u>) yours.

2. Mike lives in (the same town / the same town as) Kathy.

3. Mike's and Ted's cars are (similar / similar to).

4. Teenage culture is (different from / different) adult culture.

5. Rugby is not (the same / the same as) football. Rugby is (different / different from) football.

Comparatives

- 두 명의 사람 또는 두 개의 사물(동물)을 놓고 서로 비교하는 말을 비교급이라고 해요. 우리말에는 '더 ~하다'라는 말을 붙여 쓸 수 있지만 영어는 이렇게 정해진 말이 없어요. 그래서 형용사나 부사의 끝에 보통 -er을 붙여서 각각 '더 ~한', '더 ~하게'라는 의미를 나타내고 '~보다'라는 의미의 than을 비교하는 대상 앞에 써서 비교급을 만들어요.

Short Adjective/Adverb + -er Than	More + Longer Adjective + Than / More + -ly Adverb + Than

Tom is taller than Ava. Ava can write Korean better than him.	Shannon's car is more expensive than mine. I drive more carefully than her.

	Adjective	Comparative	Adjective	Comparative
Adjective + -er	tall	taller	slow	slower
	small	smaller	short	shorter
	large	larger	cheap	cheaper
double consonant	big	bigger	thin	thinner
	fat	fatter	hot	hotter
drop -y + -ier	easy	easier	heavy	heavier
	pretty	prettier	happy	happier
For most two or more syllable adjectives, more is used.	famous	more famous	expensive	more expensive
	interesting	more interesting	difficult	more difficult

	Adjective	Comparative	Adverb	Comparative
More is used with adverbs that end in -ly.	slowly	more slowly	quickly	more quickly
	loudly	more loudly	beautifully	more beautifully
Adverb + -(e)r	fast	faster	hard	harder
	late	later		

	Adjective	Comparative	Adverb	Comparative
Irregular	good	better	well	better
	bad	worse	badly	worse

A Complete the sentences as in the example.

1. She isn't tall. You're ____taller than her____.

2. I don't work hard. You work _____.

3. The moon isn't big. The sun is _____.

4. Amy isn't pretty. You're _____.

5. Your brother isn't powerful. My brother is _____.

6. My boyfriend isn't popular. Courtney's boyfriend is _____.

Learn & Practice 3

As...As and Not As...As

- 두 명의 사람 또는 사물이 서로 같거나 비슷하다고 표현하는 말을 동등 비교라고 해요. taller처럼 비교급을 만들지 않고 원래의 형태인 tall을 as와 as 사이에 쓴다고 해서 원급 비교라고도 해요. as + 형용사/부사 + as는 '～만큼 …하다'라고 해석해요.

- 두 명의 사람이나 사물이 서로 같지 않다는 말을 할 때에는 'not as + 형용사/부사 + as'를 써서 '～만큼 …하지 않다'라고 해석해요. not as...as는 비교급(-er than)으로 바꾸어 쓸 수 있어요. 하지만 not as...as가 더 공손한(예의 바른) 느낌을 전달해요.

Karen is 170 cm. Anna is 167 cm.
Karen is **as** beautiful **as** Anna.
Anna is **not as** tall **as** Karen.
Anna is short**er than** Karen.
= Karen is tall**er than** Anna.

A Complete the sentences with as...as.

1. My grandfather ____is as old as____ my grandmother.   old

2. A tiger is _____ a lion.   dangerous

3. Jason isn't _____ his brother.   intelligent

4. You can speak English _____ I (can).   well

5. He worked _____ his boss.   hard

A Look at the pictures and prompts. Make sentences using the comparative form.

1.

the village / quiet / the city

The village is quieter than the city.

2.

the train / slow / the plane

_____

3.

the yellow car / modern / the red car

_____

4.

Korea / small / Japan

_____

B Make sentences with *(not) the same...as* using the words given.

1. a soccer ball / a tennis ball (size)

→ *A soccer ball isn't the same size as a tennis ball.*

2. a golf player / a basketball player (height)

→ _____

3. a soccer ball / a volleyball (shape)

→ _____

4. an amateur athlete / a professional athlete (ability, have)

→ _____

C Rewrite these sentences so that they have the same meaning. Use *(not) as...as*.

1. My bicycle is old. Your bicycle is old, too.

→ *My bicycle is as old as your bicycle.*

2. Bob got home late. Susan got home late, too.

→ _____

3. A river isn't big. An ocean is very big.

→ _____

4. Kathy didn't study very hard. Lucy studied very hard.

→ _____

D Complete the sentences to make correct statements as in the example.

1. is faster than → *A car is faster than a bicycle.*

2. is slower than... → _____

3. ...is more expensive than... → _____

4. ...is as fast as... → _____

5. ...is not as convenient as... → _____

6. ...is more dangerous than... → _____

7. ...more famous than... → _____

8. ...not as easy as... → _____

E Look at the pictures. Make six sentences as in the example. Use *same*, *similar*, or *different*.

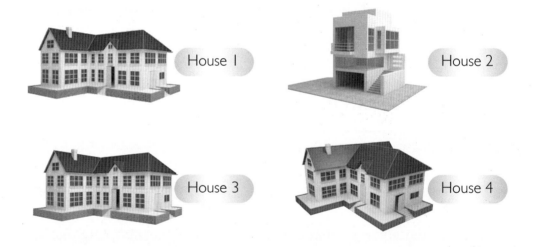

House 1

House 2

House 3

House 4

1. *House 2 is different from all the other houses.*

2. _____

3. _____

4. _____

5. _____

6. _____

A Look at the example and practice with a partner. Use the words below or invent your own. (Then change roles and practice again.)

I.

Jenny / Eric / height / ?
→ No / tall

I.

 Is Jenny the same height as Eric?

 No, Jenny isn't the same height as Eric. She is taller.

2.

Bob / his wife / weight / ?
→ No / fat

3.

men's shoe / women's shoe / size / ?
→ No / big

4.

the car / the bicycle / price / ?
→ No / cheap

B Work with a partner. Take turns making sentences using -er/more with the given words. Discuss with your partner.

Mt. Kilimanjaro / high / Mt. Fuji
basketball / popular / soccer
the Atlantic Ocean / deep / the Pacific Ocean
the giraffe / fast / the horse
Love / important / money

I think love is more important than money.

I agree. / I don't agree. I think...

C Work with a partner. Choose one of the categories below, and compare two examples from this category. Make three sentences using any types of comparative methods.

1. countries
2. cities
3. sports
4. athletes
5. schools
6. teachers
7. animals
8. languages
9. types of transportation

A plane is different from a train in many ways. A plane is more convenient than a train, in my opinion. A train isn't as fast as a plane.

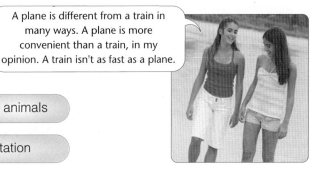

Unit 16 Comparison 2

Unit Focus
▶ Similarity with *Like* and *Alike*
▶ Superlatives
▶ *One Of The* + Superlative + Plural Noun

Learn & Practice 1

Similarity with *Like* and *Alike*

- like를 전치사로 쓰면 반드시 뒤에 명사가 와서 'be + like + 명사'의 어순으로 써요. alike는 형용사로 쓰여 반드시 be 동사 뒤에 위치한 'be + alike'로 써야 해요. 'be + like'는 '~와 비슷하다'라는 뜻이고, alike는 '비슷한'이란 뜻으로 해석해요.
- be 동사 대신에 look, sound, smell, taste, feel, seem, act, sing, dress, think 등의 동사를 쓸 수 있어요. 동사 뒤에 명사를 쓰려면 반드시 전치사 like를 써야 한다는 것을 잊지 마세요.
- look like는 '~처럼 보이다'라는 뜻으로 사람의 신체적인 외모를 나타내는 반면에, be + like는 눈에 보이는 사람의 외모 보다는 내적인 특성을 나타낼 때 자주 써요.

A football player **looks like** a soccer player.
A football player and a soccer player **look alike**.
A soccer player doesn't **dress like** a football player.
A soccer player and a football player don't **dress alike**.

Sam and I have similar phones.
In others words, his phone **is like** mine.
Our phones **are alike**.

Ⓐ Complete the sentences with *like* and *alike*.

1.

Your shopping bag is ___like___ my shopping bag.
Your shopping bag and my shopping bag ___are alike___.

2.

Eric and Bob have similar scooters. In oth words, their scooters are _____.

3.

A bus is _____ a train in some ways.

4.

These girls are sisters. She dresses _____ her sister.

Superlatives

- 최상급은 셋 이상의 사람, 사물(동물)을 비교할 때 써요. 우리말에는 '가장 ~한'이란 말을 붙여 쓸 수 있지만 영어는 이렇게 정해진 말이 없어서 형용사나 부사의 끝에 보통 -est를 붙여서 '가장 ~한'이란 뜻을 나타내요. 최상급 앞에는 정관사 the를 써요.

- "내 여자 친구가 가장 예뻐."라고 하면 예쁜 건 알겠는데, 우리 학교에서 제일 예쁜지, 아니면 전 세계를 통틀어서 제일 예쁜 건지 구체적인 범위를 정해 주면 명쾌해지겠죠. 그래서 최상급 뒤에 '~에서'를 뜻하는 전치사 in을 써서 in the world, in this class, in my family, in Korea 등을 자주 쓰고, '~중에서'라는 뜻의 전치사 of를 써서 of (all) the students, of all the cities, of all 등도 자주 써요.

Superlative: -est	Superlative: *Most*

A cheetah is **the fastest** animal **in** the world.	Seth is **the most** intelligent **of** the three brothers.

Spelling Rules of the Superlative Forms

	Adjective	Comparative	Superlative
One-syllable adjectives + **-est**	tall large cheap long	tall**er** larg**er** cheap**er** long**er**	the tall**est** the larg**est** the cheap**est** the long**est**
double consonant + **-est**	big hot thin	big**ger** hot**ter** thin**ner**	the big**gest** the hot**test** the thin**nest**
drop **-y** + **-iest**	easy heavy pretty happy	eas**ier** heav**ier** prett**ier** happ**ier**	the eas**iest** the heav**iest** the prett**iest** the happ**iest**
For most two or more syllable adjectives, **most** is used.	difficult famous popular interesting	**more** difficult **more** famous **more** popular **more** interesting	the **most** difficult the **most** famous the **most** popular the **most** interesting

	Adjective (Adverb)	Comparative	Superlative
Irregular	good (well) bad/ill (badly) many/much little	**better** **worse** **more** **less**	**the best** **the worst** **the most** **the least**

A Complete the sentences with superlatives and the appropriate preposition, *in* or *of*.

1. What is ___the highest___ (high) mountain ___in___ Korea?

2. Dennis can run _____ (fast) _____ them all.

3. Jupiter is _____ (big) planet _____ the solar system.

4. The Nile is _____ (long) river _____ Africa.

5. The new book is _____ (interesting) _____ all.

6. In my opinion, this restaurant is _____ (good) one _____ town.

7. The Mediterranean is _____ (large) sea _____ the world.

Learn & Practice 3

One Of The + Superlative + Plural Noun

- one 아는 '~의 하나'라는 뜻이므로 one of 뒤에 최상급이 올 때에는 '가장 ~한 것 중의 하나'라는 뜻이 돼요. 여러 명 (개) 중에서 한 명(하나)을 나타내므로 최상급 뒤에 오는 명사는 반드시 복수 명사를 써야 해요.

The United States of America is **one of the richest** count**ries** in the world.

He is **one of the most** successful musicians in the city.

A Complete the sentences as in the example. Use *one of the* + superlative form.

1. Air pollution is ___one of the most serious problems___ (serious problem) in Korea.

2. Andre Kim was _____ (famous fashion designer) in the world.

3. The actress is _____ (pretty woman) in the world.

4. Paris is _____ (beautiful city) in the world.

5. Today is _____ (hot day) this summer.

A Look at the pictures. Write sentences with superlatives of the words in brackets.

1.    2.    3.    4.

1. The blue whale is the biggest of all animals.

    (the blue whale / of all animals / big)

2. _____

    (the giraffe / in the world / tall animal)

3. _____

    (the ostrich / in the world / big bird)

4. _____

    (the Pluto / from the sun / far planet)

B Write sentences using the prompts and *one of the* + superlative + plural noun.

1. Korea / interesting country / to visit

→ Korea is one of the most interesting countries to visit.

2. Seoul / important city / in Korea

→ _____

3. The Grand Canyon / beautiful place / in the world

→ _____

4. The Yangtze River / long river / in Asia

→ _____

5. The Han River / great historical significance / of Korea

→ _____

6. Rolls Royce / expensive car / in the world

→ _____

C Make two sentences each with the following prompts, as in the example. Use *like* and *alike*.

1. look / a soccer player / a rugby player
   → A soccer player looks like a rugby player.
   → A soccer player and a rugby player look alike.

2. taste / Pepsi / Coke
   → _____
   → _____

3. not dress / a football player / a rugby player
   → _____
   → _____

4. not look / a Korean classroom / a classroom in another country
   → _____
   → _____

D Look at the information about the three girls below and expand the notes into sentences.

Alice	Ava	Jenny
12 years old	15 years old	15 years old
140 cm	165 cm	160 cm
30 kg	53 kg	50 kg

1. Ava / tall / of the three   → Ava is the tallest girl of the three.

2. Alice / short / Jenny   → Alice is shorter than Jenny.

3. Jenny / old / Ava   → _____

4. Alice / short girl / of the three → _____

5. Ava / heavy girl / of the three   → _____

6. Ava / heavy / Alice   → _____

7. Ava / tall / Jenny   → _____

8. Alice / young girl / of the three → _____

A Look at the example and practice with a partner. Use the words below or invent your own. (Then change roles and practice again).

1.

 In your opinion, what is one of the biggest problems in the world?

 I think hunger is one of the biggest problems in the world.

1. big problem / in the world / ?
→ hunger

2. big city / in Asia / ?
→ Tokyo

3. big problem / in Korea / ?
→ crime

4. beautiful place / in the world / ?
→ Venice

5. famous landmark / in Korea / ?
→ the Seoul Tower

6. important invention / in the twentieth century / ?
→ the Internet

B Work with a partner. Look at the jobs below and take turns to make sentences using the words in the box.

photographer

I think that the job of a bus driver is more interesting than the job of a farmer. What do you think?

I think that the job of a bus driver is the most boring.

doctor

journalist

farmer

bus driver

soldier

archaeologist

boring	exciting
difficult	dangerous
easy	interesting
well-paid	tiring

Gerunds and Infinitives 1

▶ Gerund as Subject and Object
▶ Infinitive as Subject and Object
▶ Verb + Gerund or Infinitive
▶ Infinitive of Purpose / Verb + Object + Infinitive

Learn & Practice 1

Gerund as Subject and Object

- 주어 자리와 목적어 자리에 명사나 대명사를 쓰지만 동작의 내용을 나타낼 때에는 동명사(v-ing)를 써요.

- 동명사만을 목적어로 가지는 동사가 따로 있어요.

Eating *fast food* is bad for your health.
Most children enjoy **eating** *fast food*.

Verb		+	Object
enjoy	finish		
give up	keep		
mind	avoid	+	**verb + -ing**
stop	put off		
quit	dislike		

A Complete the sentences using the words given, as in the example.

1. _Learning_ (learn) English is important.

2. She enjoys _____ (jog) at night.

3. I finished _____ (clean) my room.

4. _____ (dance) salsa was interesting.

Learn & Practice 2

Infinitive as Subject and Object

- 부정사가 주어로 쓰일 때에는 주어가 길어지기 때문에 현대 영어에서는 주로 주어 자리에 it을 쓰고 to 부정사를 뒤로 보내요.

- 부정사가 목적어 자리에서 동작을 나타낼 때 부정사만을 목적어로 가지는 동사가 따로 있어요.

To get a *good job* is hard these days.
= It is hard these days **to get** a *good job*.
Ava *hopes* **to get** a good job.

Verb		+	Object
want	expect		
would like	need		
decide	plan	+	**to + base verb**
hope	promise		
refuse	seem		
wish	agree		

A Complete the sentences with *It is* + adjective + infinitive.

1. ___It___ is always exciting ___to go___ (go) to an amusement park.

2. _____ isn't easy at all _____ (lose weight).

3. _____ is important _____ (save) energy.

4. _____ is not always difficult _____ (study) a foreign language.

B Read and underline the correct form.

1. They refused to sell / selling alcohol to teenagers.

2. The students decided to study / studying for an exam.

3. She enjoys to travel / traveling to different countries.

4. Ashley decided to quit to learn / learning to tap dance.

5. I avoided to visit / visiting his house because he had a wild dog in his yard.

6. I want to come / coming in first in the marathon race.

Learn & Practice 3

Verb + Gerund or Infinitive
- 다음과 같은 동사들은 목적어로 동명사와 to 부정사를 둘 다 쓸 수 있어요. 해석도 같고 의미 차이도 거의 없기 때문에 구별 없이 쓸 수 있어요.

Some children *hate* **to go** to school.
Some children *hate* **going** to school.

like	love	start	continue
hate	can't stand		

＊ *like*와 *love* 뒤에는 동명사와 부정사를 모두 쓸 수 있지만 **would like**와 **would love**는 목적어로 반드시 부정사를 써야 해요. (*I would like/love* ***to go...***)

A Complete the sentences with the *gerund* or *infinitive* of the verb in brackets.

1. I like ___to work / working___ (work) with computers.

2. The girl began _____ (sing).

3. I would love _____ (play) a game of chess right now.

4. It started _____ (snow) around midnight.

Infinitive of Purpose / Verb + Object + Infinitive

- 동사가 나타내는 행동이나 동작의 뜻에 더욱 구체적인 목적이나 이유(Why someone does something.)를 나타내기 위하여 부정사를 써요. 우리말로 '~하기 위하여'라고 해석해요. in order to를 쓰기도 하는데 일상 영어에서는 in order를 거의 쓰지 않고 to + base form of the verb만 써요.
- '~하기 위하여'라는 to 부정사의 목적의 의미를 'for + 명사'로도 나타낼 수 있어요.

Eric wanted to eat lunch, so he went to the cafeteria.
→ He *went* to the cafeteria **to eat** lunch.
→ He *went* to the cafeteria **in order to** eat lunch.
→ He *went* to the cafeteria **for** lunch.

- 남에게 어떤 동작이나 행동을 하길 원할 때 목적어 바로 뒤에 부정사를 써서 '동사 + 목적어 + to 부정사'로 나타내요. '(목적어)가 ~하는 것/~하라고'라는 뜻으로 해석이 되어 앞으로 해야 할 일이나 미래의 일을 내포하고 있으므로 주로 충고나 명령에 관련된 동사와 함께 자주 써요.

The teacher **wants** us **to learn** English.

Verb		Infinitive
advise, allow, ask, encourage, order, want (would like), persuade, permit, teach, tell, warn	+ Object +	to + base verb

---

A Complete the sentences with *to* or *for*.

1. I go to school __to__ learn English.
2. We use the Internet _____ do research.
3. She went to the cafeteria _____ lunch.
4. We need a dictionary _____ vocabularies.
5. He's studying _____ pass the test.

B Put the words in brackets into the correct form.

1. The teacher told ___us to write___ (we / write) an essay about our dream job.
2. My father asked _____ (I / call) my grandmother.
3. I warned _____ (she / not drive) so quickly because of the ice.
4. We persuaded _____ (Michelle / come) to the party.
5. He ordered _____ (I / leave) the library immediately.

A Rewrite the sentences with the same meaning by using *it* + infinitive.

1. To keep your own style is better.
   → It is better to keep your own style.

2. To exercise daily and not to skip breakfast is important.
   → _____

3. Not to eat too much of any one food is important.
   → _____

4. To hear one of your old stories is always interesting.
   → _____

B Look at the pictures and make sentences using the prompts as in the example. Use a *gerund* or an *infinitive*.

1.

   Kathy / enjoy / eat healthy food

   → Kathy enjoys eating healthy food. _____

2.

   I / hope / travel by train

   → _____

3.

   Bruno / want / become a pilot

   → _____

4.

   my mother / often put off / wash the dishes

   → _____

5.

   Kevin / would like / drink orange juice

   → _____

6.

   Tom / avoid / fight with his brother

   → _____

C Answer *why* questions as in the example. Show purpose by using an infinitive.

1.

eat / a hamburger

Q: Tiffany went to the fastfood restaurant. Why?

A: *She went to the fastfood restaurant to eat a hamburger.*

2.

buy / some books

Q: Ava needs to go to the bookstore. Why?

A: _____

_____

3.

see / the ancient pyramids

Q: They went to Egypt. Why?

A: _____

_____

4.

get / some fresh air

Q: Tim and Olivia took a walk in the park. Why?

A: _____

_____

D Rewrite the sentences using the verbs provided. Use object + infinitive.

1. The doctor said to me, "Stay in bed for a few days." (tell)

→ *The doctor told me to stay in bed for a few days.*

2. The teacher said to her, "Tell me the truth." (tell)

→ _____

3. Olivia said to William, "You should wash your feet." (persuade)

→ _____

4. The doctor said to him, "Stop smoking." (advise)

→ _____

5. She said to us, "Don't knock on the door loudly. (warn)

→ _____

6. Jessica said to Maria, "Stay at my house on Saturday night." (invite)

→ _____

A Look at the example and practice with a partner. Use the words below or invent your own. (Then change roles and practice again.)

1.

> Which is cheaper, to go to a movie or to rent a video?
>
> It's cheaper to go to a movie than to rent a video.
>
> I don't agree. I think that renting a video is cheaper than going to a movie.

1.
cheap: to go to a movie or to rent a video?

2.
easy: to make money or to spend money

3.
interesting: to study at the library or to go to a concert?

4.
comfortable: to wear shoes or to go barefoot?

B Work with a partner. Ask and answer questions as in the example.

Seoul /
the Seoul Tower

New York /
the Empire State Building

Why are you going to Seoul?

I'm going to Seoul to see the Seoul Tower.

Your turn to ask!

Australia /
the Sydney Opera House

Italy /
the Leaning Tower of Pisa

Paris /
the Louvre Museum

Rome /
the Colosseum

New York /
the Statue of Liberty

London /
Big Ben

Paris /
the Eiffel Tower

Unit Focus
- ► Preposition + Gerund / *Go* + *-ing*
- ► Adjective + Infinitive
- ► *Be Used To* + Gerund
- ► Using Infinitives with *Too* and *Enough*

Learn & Practice 1

Preposition + Gerund / *Go* + *-ing*

- 전치사 뒤에는 명사나 대명사를 쓰지만 동작의 내용이 오면 동명사(-ing form)를 써야 해요. 명사처럼 전치사의 목적어 역할을 하므로 우리말로 '~것(을)'이라고 해석해요.

She is interested **in climbing** rocks.

Prepositions Following Verbs/Adjectives		
fond **of**	worry **about**	interested **in**
apologize **for**	insist **on**	believe **in**
care **about**	succeed **in**	think **about**
good **at**	tired **of**	excited **about**
feel **like**	responsible **for**	look forward **to**

- '~하러 가다'라는 뜻의 'go + 동명사(v-ing)'는 주로 운동이나 레저에 많이 써요. go 뒤에 방향을 나타내는 전치사 to를 쓰면 안 돼요.

I **went fishing** with my dad yesterday.

Go		-ing	
go	+	camping	fishing
		shopping	hiking
		jogging	bowling
		sightseeing	sailing
		skating	swimming

Ⓐ **Choose the correct word.**

1. She is afraid of (flying / to fly).

2. I'm not good (at / of) speaking English.

3. He is tired of (work / working) weekends.

4. I apologize for (being / to be) late.

Ⓑ **Look at the pictures and complete the sentences. Use *go* + *-ing*.**

1.

sail

We want to ___*go*___ ___*sailing*___ this afternoon.

2.

swim

Kathy _____ yesterday.

3.

shop

Anne _____ once a week.

Adjective + Infinitive

- to 부정사가 형용사 뒤에서 형용사(easy, difficult, dangerous, hard, etc.)를 꾸밀 때 '～하기에'라는 뜻이 돼요. 감정을 나타내는 형용사(happy, glad, sad, sorry, pleased, surprised, excited, disappointed, etc.)를 꾸밀 때에는 '～해서, ～하게 되어서'라는 뜻으로 감정의 원인을 나타내요.

This article about unemployment is *difficult* **to understand**.

She was *shocked* **to hear** the news.

Ⓐ Read and complete the sentences as in the example.

1. I was pleased. + I could see Amy again. → I was pleased ___*to see*___ Amy again.

2. I'm really happy. + I can give you a hand. → I'm really happy _____ you a hand.

3. Jenny was surprised. She got Kevin's letter.
   → Jenny was surprised _____ Kevin's letter.

Be Used To + Gerund

- 'be used to + v-ing'는 'v-ing 하는 것에 익숙하다'라는 뜻으로 반드시 to 뒤에는 동명사를 써야 해요. 'be accustomed to + v-ing'도 같은 의미로 사용해요. 여기에서도 to는 전치사이므로 동명사를 써야 합니다.
- 'used to + 동사 원형'은 '～하곤 했(었)다'라는 뜻으로 지금은 하지 않지만 과거에 했던 반복된 행동을 나타내는 전혀 다른 표현이므로 be used to + v-ing와는 구별해서 사용해야 해요.

Elena **is used to** us**ing** chopsticks, but it was difficult at the beginning.
(= Elena **is accustomed** to us**ing**...)

Most people **used to walk** or **ride** horses.
Today they drive cars.

(A) Complete the sentences with *be used to* or *used to*.

1. I live in the country. I _____am not used to living_____ (not / live) in the city.

2. Steve quit jogging two years ago. He _____ (jog) four miles a day.

3. We _____ (go) to the beach every weekend, but now we don't.

4. It was difficult at first, but Sarah _____ (eat) kimchi.

5. I can't concentrate. I _____ (not / work) in such a noisy office.

Using Infinitives with *Too* and *Enough*

- 'too + 형용사 + to 부정사'는 '~하기에는 너무 ~한'이라는 뜻이에요. to 부정사를 '~하기에'로 해석하고 too는 '너무'라는 뜻으로 '어려움이나 문제가 있어 불가능하다'라는 부정의 의미를 내포하고 있어요.
- '형용사 + enough + to 부정사'는 '~할 정도로'라는 뜻이에요. enough는 형용사 뒤에 써야 하고 긍정의 의미를 내포하고 있어요.
- enough 뒤에 명사를 쓸 경우 이때의 enough는 뒤에 있는 명사를 꾸며 주며 '충분한'이라는 뜻이 되고, 'enough + 명사 + to 부정사'에서 부정사는 우리말로 '~할'이라는 뜻으로 앞에 있는 명사를 꾸며 주어요.

Ava was **too tired to walk** home.

He is **old enough to watch** the movie.

Kathy has **enough money to buy** the car.

(A) Complete the sentences with *too* or *enough* and the adjective in brackets.

1. He is _____too nervous_____ to sleep. (nervous)

2. She is _____ to buy the company. (rich)

3. The boat wasn't _____ for us to ride. (big)

4. There aren't _____ for everybody to sit down. (chairs)

5. You are _____ to go to the concert alone. (young)

6. The shirt is _____ for him to wear. (dirty)

A Combine the two sentences to make one, using adjective + infinitive.

1. You're going to the concert. Are you happy?

   → *Are you happy to go to the concert?*

2. Steve bought a new smartphone yesterday. He was delighted.

   →

3. You met your first love in Italy. Were you surprised?

   →

4. You heard the news. Were you sad?

   →

5. Elizabeth took the train without a ticket. She was wrong.

   →

B Look at the pictures and write sentences using *too/enough* as in the example.

1.

   Sue is strong enough, so she can carry the suitcase.

   → *Sue is strong enough to carry the*

   suitcase.

2.

   Sam is too busy, so he can't go to the party.

   →

3.

   Cody has enough money, so he can buy the ties.

   →

4.

   Peter was too tired, so he couldn't wash the dishes.

   →

C Read these situations and write two sentences with *used to*, as in the example.

1. Yongjae is Korean. He went to Japan and found driving on the right difficult.
   → At first he _____ *wasn't used to driving on the right* _____ .
   → Now he has no problems. He _____ *is used to driving on the right* _____ .

2. Julie is American. She went to Korea. When she first ate some food, she found it very difficult because she had to use chopsticks. Using them was strange and difficult at first.
   → At first she _____ .
   → Now she finds it normal. She _____ .

3. Carmen is a nurse. She started working nights two years ago. At first she found it difficult and didn't like it.
   → At first she _____ .
   → Now she doesn't mind it at all. She _____ .

D Complete the sentences as in the example. Use prepositions and gerunds.

1. Lisa likes to learn about other countries and cultures. She's interested in that.
   → She's interested ___ *in learning* ___ about other countries and cultures.

2. Sarah wants to go out to eat just because she feels like it.
   → She feels _____ out to eat.

3. The children are going to go to Lottle World. They're excited about that.
   → The children are excited _____ to Lottle World.

E Look at the pictures and the prompts. Write questions and answers, as in the example.

1.

Q: *Does Mark like to go snowboarding?*
A: *No, he doesn't. He likes to go jogging.*

Mark / snowboarding / ?
→ No / jogging

2.

Q: _____
A: _____

Kevin / skydiving / ?
→ No / scuba diving

A Look at the example and practice with a partner. Use the words below or invent your own. (Then change roles and practice again.)

I.

 Why can't Kristen wear the jeans? They are too tight for her to wear.

1.
Kristen / wear / the jeans / ?
→ tight

2.
Tom / finish / his homework / ?
→ sleepy

3.
they / lift / the sofa / ?
→ heavy

4.
Kelly / eat / the pizza / ?
→ hot

5.

 Let's go skydiving. Yes, I have enough time to go skydiving.

5.
skydiving

6.
skiing

7.
camping

8.
shopping

B Work with a partner. Answer each question with a complete sentence. Use *be used to* + gerund or noun.

1. What are you used to drinking in the morning?
2. What kind of food are you used to (eating)?
3. What kind of weather are you used to?
4. What time are you used to getting up?
5. What kinds of clothes are you used to wearing to class / work?
6. What kinds of things are you used to doing every day?
7. What kinds of things are you used to doing alone?

What are you used to drinking in the morning?

I'm used to drinking milk in the morning.

Your turn to ask!

Conjunctions

▶ The Conjunctions: *And*, *But*, and *Or*
▶ The Conjunctions: *So* and *Because*
▶ *Too*, *So*, *Either*, and *Neither*

Learn & Practice 1

The Conjunctions: *And*, *But*, and *Or*

- and, but, or는 문장과 문장을 서로 연결해 주는 역할을 해요. 문장과 문장을 연결할 때에는 접속사 바로 앞에 comma(,)를 써요.

- and(그리고, ~와)는 다른 문장에 추가적인 정보를 주는 역할을 하고, but(그러나, 하지만)은 서로 반대되거나 대조적인 뜻을 담고 있어요. or(또는, 혹은)는 어느 하나를 선택하게끔 하는 역할을 합니다.

I saw the doctor, **and** he gave me a prescription.

She usually takes a subway to work, **but** she drove this morning.

Tom will go fishing, **or** he will go scuba diving.

- and, but, or가 두 개의 단어(즉, two nouns, two adjectives, two adverbs, etc.)를 연결할 때에는 comma(,)를 쓰지 않고 세 개 이상의 단어를 연결할 때 각 단어 뒤와 접속사 앞에 comma(,)를 써요. 단, and 앞에서는 comma(,)를 쓰기도 하고 안 쓰기도 해요.

- 주어가 동일하여 접속사 뒤에 나오는 똑같은 주어를 생략할 때에는 접속사 앞에 comma(,)를 쓰지 않아요.

Jane puts milk, sugar, **and** kiwi in her tea.

Jane puts milk, sugar **and** kiwi in her tea.

Do you want iced tea **or** hot tea?

I want some bread **and** orange juice.

I went to bed, **but** I couldn't sleep.

I went to bed **but** couldn't sleep.

Ⓐ Complete the sentences with *and*, *but*, or *or*. Add commas if necessary.

1. I washed my shirt. _____but_____ it didn't get clean.

2. We should finish this project_____ then go home.

3. I tried to visit you many times_____ you were not home.

4. It's not easy to understand other cultures_____ at least you should try.

5. Do you like milk_____ orange juice?

6. I bought some paper, a greeting card_____ some envelopes.

The Conjunctions: *So* and *Because*

- so는 '그래서, 그러므로'라는 뜻으로 앞에는 원인, 뒤에는 결과를 나타내는 역할을 해요. 문장과 문장만을 연결하고 반드시 so 앞에는 comma(,)를 써야 해요.
- because는 '~ 때문에, 왜냐하면'이라는 뜻으로 중심 문장(주절)에 대한 이유나 원인을 나타내요. 의문사 why에 대한 대답으로 because를 써요.

Jennifer stayed up all night, **so** she was very tired.

We don't trust her **because** she made a big mistake.

A Complete the sentences with *so* or *because*. Add commas where necessary.

1. He has lost his glasses, _____so_____ he can't see anything.

2. All his friends have gone on holiday_____ he is very bored and doesn't know what to do.

3. We opened the window_____ it was very hot.

4. Linda is very hungry_____ she didn't have breakfast.

5. They had some free time_____ they went to the movies.

Too, So, Either, and Neither

- 앞서 말한 상대방 의견에 동의하여 앞 문장이 긍정일 때 'so + 동사(do 동사 / be 동사 / 조동사) + 주어'를 써서 '~도 또한 그렇다'라는 뜻을 나타내요. 앞 문장이 부정 의견인 부정문일 때에는 'neither + 동사(do 동사 / be 동사 / 조동사) + 주어'로 써서 '~도 또한 아니다'라는 표현을 만들 수 있어요.

Scott has curly hair.	**So does I.** = I do too. = Me too. = I have curly hair, too.
He doesn't have straight hair.	**Neither do I.** = I don't either. = Me neither. = I don't have straight hair, either.
He is a student.	**So am I.** = I am too. = Me too. = I am a student, too.

＊Me too와 Me neither는 주로 일상 영어(informal spoken English)에서 많이 써요.

- be 동사와 조동사는 그대로 쓰고 일반 동사일 경우에는 do(does, did)를 써요.

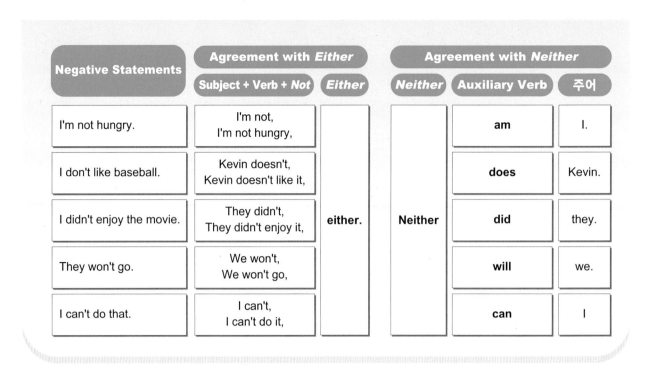

Negative Statements	Agreement with *Either*		Agreement with *Neither*		
	Subject + Verb + *Not*	*Either*	*Neither*	Auxiliary Verb	주어
I'm not hungry.	I'm not, I'm not hungry,			am	I.
I don't like baseball.	Kevin doesn't, Kevin doesn't like it,			does	Kevin.
I didn't enjoy the movie.	They didn't, They didn't enjoy it,	either.	Neither	did	they.
They won't go.	We won't, We won't go,			will	we.
I can't do that.	I can't, I can't do it,			can	I

A Write sentences showing agreement using *so* or *neither*. Use *I*.

1. I am hungry.

2. I enjoy skiing.

3. I didn't go to the party last night.

4. I don't like doing homework.

5. I can swim very well.

6. I haven't read this book.

7. I will go shopping tomorrow.

8. I went to the park yesterday.

So am I.
_____

_____

_____

_____

_____

_____

_____

_____

A Join the sentences by putting in a conjunction. Use *and, but, or, so,* or *because.*

1. I stayed at home. I watched the TV.
   → I stayed at home, and I watched the TV. / I stayed at home and watched the TV.

2. It was very hot. We opened the window.
   →

3. The teenage girls will go on a picnic. They will go to the amusement park.
   →

4. Tom is foolish. His brother is wise.
   →

5. My stomachache was really bad. I took some medicine for it.
   →

6. I go to the restaurant. The waiter is really handsome.
   →

7. We didn't have class. The teacher was absent.
   →

8. The flight attendants served dinner. I didn't eat.
   →

B Write at least 6 sentences using *and, or, but, so,* or *because.*

1. We need to eat fruit and vegetables for good health.

2. I waved at my friend, but she didn't see me.

3.

4.

5.

6.

7.

8.

C Rewrite the sentences using *so* or *neither*.

1. Steve likes playing soccer. His brother likes it, too.

   → *Steve likes playing soccer, and so does his brother.* _____

2. Ava won't go to the movies. Sophia won't go, either.

   → _____

3. I enjoyed my holidays very much. Matt also enjoyed his holidays.

   → _____

4. Kevin eats too much junk food. You eat it, too.

   → _____

D Complete the sentences with an auxiliary verb + *too* or *either*.

1.

my wife

I can't cook, and ___*my wife can't either*___.

2.

my roommate

I like scary movies, and _____
_____.

3.

my brother

I don't like salty food, and _____
_____.

4.

pasta

Pizza is a famous Italian dish, and _____
_____.

5.

anteaters

Most birds don't have teeth, and
_____.

6.

tortoises

Snakes are reptiles, and _____
_____.

118 Unit 19

A Look at the example and practice with a partner. Use the words below or invent your own. (Then change roles and practice again.)

1.

> What do you have to do at home?
>
> I have to babysit my sister.
>
> So do I.

1. babysit / my sister
2. wash / my dad's car
3. clean / my bedroom
4. take / the trash out
5. iron / my clothes
6. water / the plants

B Work with a partner. Make sentences about George and Sarah, using *so* or *neither*.

	George	Sarah
loves baseball	No	No
cooks every day	Yes	Yes
likes K-pop music	Yes	Yes
is working this Saturday	No	No
has already been to Korea	Yes	Yes
goes to the gym quite often	Yes	Yes
watched TV yesterday evening	Yes	Yes
can speak Korean and Japanese	No	No
went out yesterday	No	No
have a math test tomorrow	Yes	Yes

George doesn't love baseball, and neither does Sarah.

I love baseball.

So do I.

Your trun now!

Conjunctions 119

Conditional Clauses

Unit Focus

▶ Present Real (or Zero) Conditional
▶ First Type (or Future) Conditional Sentences
▶ Second Type Conditional Sentences
▶ Wishes about the Present or Future

Learn & Practice 1

Present Real (or Zero) Conditional

- 'if + 주어 + 동사…'만으로는 완전한 문장을 만들 수 없고 반드시 중심 문장(main clause)과 함께 써야 의미를 전달할 수 있어요. if가 이끄는 절(if + 주어 + 동사)은 중심 문장 앞 또는 뒤에 모두 쓸 수 있는데, if절이 문장의 앞에 올 때에는 comma(,)를 써야 해요. if가 이끄는 조건의 부사절은 '~한다면'이라는 뜻으로 뜻인 조건(condition)을 나타내고, 중심 문장(main clause)은 결과(reason)를 나타내는 역할을 해요.

- 조건을 나타내는 if절의 내용이 일반적인 사실, 일상적으로 일어나는 일 또는 정해진 상황을 나타낼 때 if절 안에는 현재 시제를 쓰고 중심 문장에도 마찬가지로 현재 시제를 써요. 이 때 if 대신 when을 쓸 수 있어요.

General Fact	Definite Thing	Everyday Thing

If (=When) the temperature **falls** below zero, water **turns** to ice.	If he **has** enough time, he **watches** TV every evening.	If I **meet** Nick on the weekend, we **go** to the movies.

If-Clause (If + Simple Present)	Main Clause (Simple Present)
If (When) you **heat** water to 100℃,	it **boils**.
Main Clause (Simple Present)	**If-Clause (If + Simple Present)**
Water **boils**	if (when) you **heat** it to 100℃.

A Complete the sentences using the verbs in brackets in the right form.

1.

If she _has_ (have) a headache, she _takes_ (take) an aspirin.

2.

If a friend _____ (tell) me a secret, I always _____ (keep) it.

3.

When it _____ (snow), people _____ (wear) warm clothes.

First Type (or Future) Conditional Sentences

- 현재나 미래에 일어날 가능성이 있는 일을 추측하거나 가정할 때 if절(if-clause) 안에 현재 시제를 쓰고 중심 문장(main clause)에는 미래 시제를 써요. 조건의 부사절인 if절이 미래를 나타내더라도 그 안에는 will 또는 be going to와 같은 미래 시제를 쓸 수 없고 반드시 현재 시제로 미래를 나타내요.
- 중심 문장(=주절)에는 will뿐만 아니라 미래를 나타내는 어떤 형태의 동사도 쓸 수 있어요.

If we **go** by bus, we **have to transfer** twice.

If you **don't give** me my money, I **'m going** to the police.

I **will wear** my raincoat to school if it **rains** tomorrow.

A Complete the sentences with the words in parentheses.

I. If I _____am_____ (be) tired this evening, I ___will stay___ (stay / will) home.

2. If he _____ (finish) his homework soon, he _____ (go / can) to bed.

Second Type Conditional Sentences

- 현재나 미래에 일어날 가능성이 적지만 10%–20% 정도의 가능성을 염두에 두고 말을 할 때 if절(if-clause)에는 과거 시제 (simple past)를 쓰고 중심 문장(main clause)에는 조동사 과거(could, would)를 써요. 이는 단순히 과거를 나타내는 표현이 아니에요. 현재나 미래에 일어날 가능성이 아주 적다는 말을 눈에 띄게 하려고 과거 시제를 쓴 것뿐이에요.

If you **saw** someone breaking into your house, what **would** you **do**?

If I **were** a police officer, I **could catch** the thief.

If-Clause			Main Clause		
If	**Subject**	**Past Tense Verb**	**Subject**	***Would/Could***	**Base Verb**
If	I/you/he/she we/they	**had** a lot of money, ***were** very rich,	I/you/he/he the/we/they	**would/could**	**buy** the house

- If 조건절에 주어의 인칭과 수에 관계없이 be 동사의 과거는 were를 써요. 주로 사람의 견해나 충고에 사용하는데, 문법을 틀려가면서까지 견해나 충고를 강조하기 위해 사용해요. 일상 영어에서는 was를 쓰기도 하지만 were가 더 자연스러운 표현으로 많이 써요.

A Complete the sentences as in the example.

1. I'm not a doctor. If I ___were/was___ a doctor, I could help sick children in Africa.

2. I don't have a camera. If I _____ a camera, I would attend the photo contest.

3. I don't know the answer. If _____ the answer, I'd tell you.

4. Alicia has a car. She couldn't travel much if she _____ a car.

5. Peter isn't in his office. Peter would answer the phone if he _____ in his office.

Learn & Practice 4

Wishes about the Present or Future

- 'wish + 과거 시제(simple past)'를 써서 현재나 미래에 대한 소망을 나타낼 수 있어요. 여기에서 과거 시제를 단순 과거로 보면 안 돼요. 현재나 미래에 대해 가능성이 적기 때문에 과거 시제를 쓰는 거예요.
- could는 현재 할 수 없는 일에 대한 후회, would는 다른 사람이 미래에 해 주길 바라는 소망을 나타낼 때 써요.
- 2차 조건문과 마찬가지로 be 동사는 were를 써요. 일상 영어에서는 was를 쓰기도 합니다.

She **wishes** she **could play** the guitar. (She cannot play the guitar.)

We **wish** he **weren't** (**wasn't**) ill now. (He is sick now.)

I **wish** you **would stop** smoking so much. (He is a heavy smoker.)

Main Clause			Noun Clause	
Subject	Wish	(That)	Subject	Past Tense Verb
I/You/We/They	wish	(that)	I/you/she/he it/we/they	Simple Past / Were (Was)
He/She/It	wish**es**			

A Write sentences about what people wish as in the example.

1. I can't speak Korean. → I wish I could speak Korean.

2. I don't know Jenny's phone number. → _____

3. Kelly doesn't have a smartphone. → _____

4. We aren't university students. → _____

A Vanessa is an actress. She doesn't like her present life. She wishes it were different. Write her wishes.

1. People follow me everywhere.
   → I wish people didn't follow me everywhere.

2. Journalists write untrue stories about me.
   → _____

3. Moviegoers touch me and pull my clothes.
   → _____

4. I have to sign autographs all the time.
   → _____

5. I can't go to the restaurant to get food.
   → _____

6. I can't wear anything I want.
   → _____

7. I don't have privacy.
   → _____

B Make sentences as in the examples.

Things You Can't Do		Your Wish
1. I can't speak English well.	→	I wish I could speak English well.
2. _____	→	_____
3. _____	→	_____
4. _____	→	_____

Things You Want to Be	Your Wish or Things You Want to Do
5. If I were a doctor,	I could help sick children in Africa.
6. _____	_____
7. _____	_____
8. _____	_____

Conditional Clauses **123**

C Make sentences with *if* as in the examples.

> I'm afraid the bus will be late.

1. get to work late again → If the bus is late, I'll get to work late again.

2. lose my job → If I get to work late again, I'll lose my job.

3. not find another job → _____

4. lose my apartment → _____

5. move back to my parents' house → _____

6. get very bored → _____

7. go fishing every day. → _____

D Join the sentences to form the present real conditional. Use the words in brackets.

1.

It's usually very hot in the summer.
Plants need lots of water. (if)

If it is very hot in the summer, plants
need lots of water.

2.

Water reaches boiling point. Then, it
changes into steam. (when)

_____

_____

3.

Sometimes you throw an apple into the air.
Then, gravity pulls it back to earth again. (if)

_____

_____

4.

I sometimes feel really tired. Then, I
usually listen to K-pop music. (if)

_____

_____

E Look at the pictures and prompts. Ask and answer questions, as in the example.

1.

order a salad /
a sandwich

Q: Shall I order a salad or a sandwich?

A: If I were you, I'd order a salad.

2.

go to Korea /
France

Q: _____

A: _____

A Look at the example and practice with a partner. Use the words below or invent your own. (Then change roles and practice again.)

1.

Do you think it will rain tomorrow?

Maybe it will rain tomorrow. If it rains tomorrow, I'm going to watch a movie on TV.

1.
it / rain / tomorrow / ?
→ watch a movie on TV

2.
it / be hot / tomorrow / ?
→ go swimming

3.
the weather / be nice / tomorrow / ?
→ go on a hike

4.
the class / be canceled / tomorrow / ?
→ go to the beach

B Work with a partner. What would you do to make the world a better place if you were one of the people below? Interview each other as in the example.

a doctor   a politician   a scientist

a teacher   a police officer

What would you do to make the world a better place if you were a doctor?

If I were a doctor, I would treat the poor people for free.

Your turn to ask!

C Work with a partner. Ask questions and answer them as in the example.

1. cut down / all forests / world's climate / change
2. not stop / use / aerosols / destroy / ozone layer
3. find / alternative sources of energy / solve / some of our environmental problems
4. temperatures / go up / by a few degrees / sea levels / rise
5. recycle / waste / save / natural resources
6. population / continue to increase / not be enough food for everyone

What will happen if we cut down all forests?

If we cut down all forests, the world's climate will change.

Your turn to ask!

You are my

Grammar & Speaking

3
Workbook

Answer Key

Unit 1
Simple Present vs. Present Progressive p. 6

Learn & Practice 1

A 2. Cindy doesn't understand Korean.
   3. We're working at my dad's shop these days.
   4. Betty usually goes swimming on the weekend.
   5. The teacher is talking to a student now.

Learn & Practice 2

A 2. hate
   3. am thinking
   4. is looking
   5. tastes

Learn & Practice 3

A 2. are going to the movies tonight
   3. is having a party next weekend
   4. is flying to Jeju Island in two hours

Super Writing

A 2. Bruno usually doing his homework, but today he is playing the guitar.
   3. Emma usually listens to music, but today she is watching a movie on TV.
   4. Steve usually takes swimming lessons, but today he is cleaning his room.
B 2. Alice is having lunch with John on Wednesday.
   3. Alice is meeting her boyfriend on Friday.
   4. Alice is seeing a scary movie with Nick on Saturday.
   5. Alice is going shopping with her mother on Sunday.
C 2. The boy is thinking about eating a biscuit.
   3. What are you looking at?
   4. Are you listening to the radio at the moment?
   5. I hate cold evenings.
   6. They're looking at clothes at the moment.
   7. We don't understand the lessons.
D 2. Is Peter watching TV at the moment? / No, he isn't. He is doing the laundry.
   3. Are Elena and Jeremy learning Chinese at school this year? / No, they aren't. They are learning Korean.
   4. Does Glen usually exercise early in the morning? / No, he doesn't. He usually rides a skateboard.

Unit 2
Simple Present vs. Simple Past p. 12

Learn & Practice 1

A 2. Did they live in Korea 5 years ago? / they did
   3. Did she answer some emails last night? / she didn't
   4. Does water boil at 100 degrees Celsius? / it does

Learn & Practice 2

A 2. does / close 3. arrives 4. does / arrive
   5. Does / take off

Learn & Practice 3

A 2. Kevin used to go fishing.
   3. I didn't use to play the guitar.
   4. We didn't use to take a taxi.
   5. Claire used to be lazy.
   6. She used to eat meat.

Super Writing

A 3. Rachel(She) drinks a lot of milk every day.
   4. Rachel(She) watched her favorite TV show yesterday.
   5. Rachel(She) brushes her teeth every day.
   6. Rachel(She) washed her clothes and dried them.
   7. Rachel(She) goes to school on foot every day.
   8. Rachel(She) baked cakes for her family yesterday.
B 2. She used to have a boyfriend, but now she is single.
   3. She used to live in the countryside, but now she lives in the city.
   4. She didn't use to talk much, but now she is more outgoing.
   5. She used to play soccer, but now she plays baseball.
   6. She didn't use to speak much Korean, but now she speaks it very well.
C 2. Does the movie start at 9:00? / No, it doesn't. It starts at 10:00.
   3. Does this semester end on March 12th? / No, it doesn't. It ends on March 15th.
   4. Does the bank close at 3:00 tomorrow? / No, it doesn't. It closes at 5:00 tomorrow.
D 2. Does Kathy talk to John on the phone? / Yes, she does.
   3. Does Jessica go to the movies? / No, she doesn't.

4. Did the girls stay at home last night? / Yes, they did.

Unit 3
Simple Past vs. Past Progressive
p. 18

Learn & Practice 1
A 2. No, she didn't. She came from the United States.
  3. No, he didn't. He loved Juliet.
  4. No, they didn't. They discovered radium.
B 2. Was it snowing last night? / it wasn't
  3. Was he studying Spanish? / he was

Learn & Practice 2
A 2. was watching / knocked
  3. were sitting / began

Learn & Practice 3
A 2. F 3. T 4. F

Super Writing
A 2. She was happy when Bob passed the exam. / When Bob passed the exam, she was happy.
  3. He never played soccer again after he broke his leg. / After he broke his leg, he never played soccer again.
  4. She went to Namsan Park as soon as she reached Seoul. / As soon as she reached Seoul, she went to Namsan Park.
B 2. Tony called while you were taking a shower.
  3. Nancy and Walter were walking in the street when it started raining.
  4. Elizabeth was watching a drama on TV when her father arrived.
  5. Ava was riding in a bus when the accident happened.
C Answers will vary.
D 2. Maybe he was changing a light bulb when he fell off the ladder.
  3. Maybe she was reading a newspaper when she heard a strange noise.
  4. They were watching a movie on TV when they fell asleep.
  5. Maybe she was going down the stairs without turning on the lights when she fell down.
  6. Maybe he was repairing the laptop when it fell and broke to pieces.

Unit 4
The Future Tense
p. 24

Learn & Practice 1
A 2. I'll 3. I'll 4. I'm going to
B 2. am about to go
  3. is about to take a picture

Learn & Practice 2
A 2. doesn't feed 3. will fail 4. drops

Learn & Practice 3
A 2. gets / gets 3. gets / listens
  4. go / will buy 5. turns / will get
  6. take / die

Super Writing
A 2. He's going to have lunch with Susan at 1 o'clock.
  3. He's going to give an interview at the NBC studio at 2 o'clock.
  4. He's going to fly to Japan at 4 o'clock.
  5. He's going to attend the Music Monthly Awards Ceremony at 6 o'clock.
B 2. Peter and Ava will go to the movie theater after they have lunch.
  3. They will wash the car before they watch their favorite show on TV.
  4. I will get married when I am 27 years old.
C 2. will 3. will 4. am going to
D 2. If you don't learn how to use a computer, you'll have trouble finding a job.
  3. If John does well in science, his parents will buy him a smartphone.
  4. If we leave now, we will probably get caught in traffic.
E 2. are about to eat at a mall
  3. is about to do the laundry
  4. is about to open the window

Unit 5
Quantifying Expressions

Learn & Practice 1
A **2.** little **3.** little **4.** few **5.** little **6.** a few

Learn & Practice 2
A **2.** many **3.** much **4.** a lot of
 5. much **6.** a lot of
B **2.** How much milk do you drink every day?
 3. How many books do you buy every month?

Learn & Practice 3
A **2.** too many / too much **3.** too many
 4. too many / too much **5.** too many
 6. too much **7.** too much

Super Writing
A **2.** Is there much butter on the table? / there is a little
    butter (on the table).
 3. Is there much money in the wallet? / there is little
    money (in the wallet).
 4. Is there much cheese on the table? / there isn't any
    cheese (on the table).
 5. Are there many eggs in the basket? / there are a
    few eggs (in the basket).
 6. Are there many cookies in the glass jar? / there are
    a few cookies (in the glass jar).
 7. Are there many tomatoes on the table? / there
    aren't any tomatoes (on the table).
 8. Is there much milk in the glass? / there is little milk
    (in the glass).
B **2.** How much suntan oil did you take with you?
 3. How much milk is there in the fridge?
 4. How many players are there on a soccer team?
C **2.** There is too much food on the table.
 3. Anna buys too much fruit at the market.
 4. There are too many cars in the city center.
D **2.** There are a few bananas in the fridge but there
    aren't any oranges.
 3. There is a little milk in the fridge but there isn't any
    yogurt.
 4. There is a little ice cream in the fridge but there
    isn't any chocolate.
 5. There are a few potatoes in the fridge but there
    aren't any carrots.

Unit 6
Expressions of Quantity
p. 36

Learn & Practice 1
A **2.** All of **3.** All
 4. All **5.** All of
B **2.** of **3.** of **4.** of
 5. × **6.** ×

Learn & Practice 2
A **2.** are **3.** are **4.** has
 5. is **6.** are **7.** is

Learn & Practice 3
A **2.** One of **3.** None of **4.** One of

Super Writing
A **2.** Almost all of the people
 3. Almost all of the people
 4. All (of) the people
 5. One of the people(women)
 6. None of the people
 7. Some of the people
 8. One of the students
 9. None of the people
 10. None of the people
 11. All (of) the students (Almost all of the people)
B **2.** No, none of them is/are wild animals.
 3. Yes, all of them are countries.
 4. No, none of them are farm animals.
 5. Yes, all of them are movie stars.
C **2.** One of my favorite soccer players is Park Jisung.
 3. None of those bags is/are mine.
 4. Most of the information is useless.
 5. None of the students in my class speak/speaks
    Korean.
 6. Almost all of the air in the city is polluted.
D **2.** All the buses run on Sundays.
 3. All the movies start at 6 o'clock.
 4. All the lessons will start on Tuesday.
 5. All the shops will be open tomorrow.
E **2.** All of them live in Africa. / None of them live/lives
    in Europe.
 3. All of them are in Korea. / None of them are/is in
    Japan.

Learn & Practice 1
A **2.** too **3.** very **4.** too **5.** too
B **2.** go swimming **3.** buy it **4.** forgive him

Learn & Practice 2
A **2.** The water is too dirty for us to drink.
  3. Steve is too young to drive a car.
  4. It is too noisy for me to sleep.
B **2.** for her to eat **3.** for me to wear
  4. for us to understand **5.** for me to carry
  6. for them to read

Learn & Practice 3
A **2.** smart enough **3.** enough money
  4. tall enough **5.** strong enough
  6. enough time **7.** enough chairs

Super Writing
A **2.** It is too crowded. **3.** He isn't tall enough.
  4. She doesn't have enough chocolate.
B **2.** too tired to go **3.** too heavy to carry
  4. tall enough to touch **5.** too hot to drink
  6. too full to hold **7.** smart enough to understand
C **2.** The waiter is too rude. He isn't polite enough.
  3. The plate is too dirty. It isn't clean enough.
  4. The meat is too tough. It isn't tender enough.
  5. The food is too expensive. It isn't cheap enough.
D **2.** The jeans are too tight. Julie can't wear them. / The jeans are very tight, but Laura can wear them.
  3. The shoes are too big. Kate can't wear them. / The shoes are very big, but Eric can wear them.
  4. The car is very expensive, but Alice can buy it. / The car is too expensive. Sarah can't buy it.
E **2.** Do you have enough money to buy a diamond ring? / No(Yes), I don't have(have) enough money to buy a diamond ring.
  3. Do you have enough time to finish your homework? / No(Yes), I don't have(have) enough time to finish my homework.
  4. Do you have enough vegetables to make five sandwiches? / No(Yes), I don't have(have) enough vegetables to make five sandwiches.

Learn & Practice 1
A **2.** anybody **3.** anything **4.** someone
  5. anywhere **6.** anybody

Learn & Practice 2
A **2.** nobody **3.** nowhere **4.** nothing

Learn & Practice 3
A **2.** it **3.** It
B **2.** them **3.** ones **4.** one **5.** it

Super Writing
A **2.** nobody **3.** something
  4. anywhere **5.** somebody
  6. anybody **7.** nowhere
  8. somewhere
B **2.** We threw away the old sofa and bought a new one.
  3. That car is fast but this one is faster.
  4. This plate is too small. Please get me a bigger one.
  5. This story is as interesting as the other ones.
  6. I don't want the blue pen. Please give me the red one.
C She went to the big clothing store near her home yesterday but didn't find anything nice. This morning she went somewhere else, but every was expensive. At another shop, everything was nice, but nothing would fit her. There's nowhere else to go. Abby is going to look in her wardrobe and find something to wear to the party.
D **2.** We can't afford this apartment. Can you show us a cheaper one?
  3. These boys are very handsome! Which ones? Can you show me again?
  4. Which shoes are yours? The ones by the window are mine.
E **2.** He said nothing about it.
  3. There is nothing in the desk drawer.
  4. There was nobody at home when I called.
  5. There was a thunderstorm during the night but I heard nothing.

Juliet was written by Shakespeare. / Was Romeo and Juliet written by Shakespeare?

Unit 9

p. 54

The Passive

Learn & Practice 1

A **2.** wrote / written **3.** painted / painted
   4. grew / grown

B **2.** The thief was caught
   3. The magazine is read
   4. This dress was designed
   5. The museum is visited

Learn & Practice 2

A **2.** That film wasn't made by Spielberg.
   3. Our mail isn't delivered by him.
   4. The office isn't cleaned every day.

B **2.** The Seoul Tower isn't visited by many people.
   3. The class isn't taught by Mr. Brown.
   4. These houses weren't built by us.
   5. Those cookies weren't made by her.

Learn & Practice 3

A **2.** Was the house built by them?
   3. Was the package mailed by Emily?
   4. Is a bird catched by a cat?
   5. Were the apples eaten by you?

Super Writing

A **2.** Is our mail delivered by Mr. Smith? / it is
   3. Are taxes collected by the government? / they are
   4. Was Derek hired by that company? / he wasn't
   5. Was Pasta introduced to Europe by Marco Polo? / it was
   6. Is the classroom cleaned by the students? / it isn't

B **2.** The movie frightens them.
   3. The waiter serves the coffee.
   4. The patient uses a wheel chair.
   5. Eric designs the hotel.
   6. Mrs. Wilson cleans the plates.

C **2.** My laptop was stolen by someone.
   3. The room was cleaned by my brother.
   4. That house was built in the middle ages by someone.

D **2.** King Sejong created Hangeul in the 15th century. / Hangeul was created in the 15th century by King Sejong. / Was Hangeul created in the 15th century by King Sejong?
   3. Shakespeare wrote Romeo and Juliet. / Romeo and

Unit 10

p. 60

Helping Verbs 1

Learn & Practice 1

A **2.** Can Mark and Paul play volleyball? / they can't
   3. Can Steve read and write? / he can
   4. Could she solve the math problem? / she couldn't
   5. Can you speak Japanese? / I can't

B **2.** can **3.** can't **4.** could **5.** couldn't

Learn & Practice 2

A **2.** In the future we will be able to go to the moon.
   3. She was able to play the piano.
   4. He isn't able to run five miles.

Learn & Practice 3

A **2.** ought to **3.** ought to **4.** ought not to
B **2.** had better **3.** had better **4.** had better not

Learn & Practice 4

A **2.** Can I **3.** May I **4.** may **5.** May I

Super Writing

A **2.** Can I invite some friends to lunch?
   3. Can I watch TV with my sister, Alexa?
   4. May I go to the toilet?
   5. May I try these(dresses) on? / May I try on these dresses?

B **2.** shouldn't speak / should speak
   3. should eat / shouldn't eat
   4. should be / shouldn't leave
   5. should wear / shouldn't use

C **2.** Jessica ought to see a doctor.
   3. You had better leave now.
   4. We ought to buy Haley a smartphone for her birthday.

E **2.** They were able to ride a bicycle in the park.
   3. Are you able to write a letter to your mother?
   4. I tried very hard, but I wasn't able to do all of my math problems.
   5. We won't be able to see him until next week.

Unit 11

Helping Verbs 2

p. 66

Learn & Practice 1

A **2.** They have to be quiet. / They have got to be quiet.
   3. You have to get her to a doctor. / You have got to get her to a doctor.

B **2.** Does she have to turn off the TV? / she does
   3. Do we have to get up early? / we don't
   4. Did he have to stay at home? / he did

Learn & Practice 2

A **2.** mustn't **3.** don't have to
   4. didn't have to **5.** mustn't

Learn & Practice 3

A **2.** possibility **3.** ability

Learn & Practice 4

A **2.** must **3.** can't

Super Writing

A **2.** It may rain today.
   3. Cindy may not change her job.
   4. Sarah may go to Korea next week.
   5. I may go to out tonight.

C **2.** Why did she go to the post office yesterday? / Because she had to post some letters.
   3. Why did they call the babysitter yesterday? / Because they had to attend a meeting.
   4. Why did she go to the hospital yesterday? / Because she had to visit a friend.

D **2.** must not work on Friday
   3. must have a pet

F **2.** You must listen to the teacher.
   3. You mustn't talk with your friend.
   4. You mustn't sleep in class.

Unit 12

Present Perfect 1

p. 72

Learn & Practice 1

A **2.** c **3.** b **4.** a **5.** d

Learn & Practice 2

A **2.** has **3.** spoken **4.** have
   5. eaten **6.** broken

Learn & Practice 3

A **2.** We haven't seen the movie.
   3. Has Eric cleaned the house?
   4. Has Linda been to Thailand?
   5. I haven't left my phone in the subway.
   6. We haven't prepared for the party.
   7. Has she ridden a horse?

Super Writing

A **2.** Tom has broken his leg.
   3. I have worked very hard for this exam.
   4. They have been married for 40 years.

B **2.** Kathy(She) has washed her hair.
   3. Scott(He) has lost weight.
   4. The car(It) has run out of gas.
   5. Kevin(He) has broken his leg.
   6. Ava(She) has gone to China.

C **2.** Has Scarlett met a famous cyclist? / No, she hasn't. She has met a famous guitarist.
   3. Has Daniel tried water skiing? / No, he hasn't. He has tried windsurfing.
   4. Have Richard and Nancy read a magazine? / No, they haven't. They have read a newspaper.

D **2.** Tara hasn't clean the kitchen.
   3. Jenny and Peter haven't watered the plants.
   4. Jack and Sally haven't done their homework.
   5. Alex hasn't fed the hamster.
   6. Tony and Ben haven't tidied up their rooms.

Unit 13

Present Perfect 2

p. 78

Learn & Practice 1

A **2.** haven't seen / since **3.** has been / for
   4. have known / since **5.** has worked / for
   6. has taught / for

Learn & Practice 2

A **2.** I have never ridden a bicycle.
   3. Have you ever climbed a mountain?
   4. Has Kate ever swum in a river?

Learn & Practice 3

A **2.** have gone **3.** has been

Learn & Practice 4

A **2.** Tom has just finished his work.

   3. They have already eaten their lunch.

   4. My brother hasn't done his homework yet.

   5. Has the plane arrived yet?

   6. They have already bought souvenirs.

Super Writing

A **2.** How long have you studied English / haven't spoken / have watched

B **2.** How long has Brad been a teacher? / She has been a teacher since 2008.

   3. How long have they worked here? / They have worked here for six months.

   4. How long has Nicole known them? / She has known them since last year.

   5. How long has Sarah been ill? / She has been ill since Saturday.

C **4.** She has written letters yet.

   5. She has just called her father.

   6. She has already cleaned her bedroom.

   7. She hasn't made sandwiches yet.

   8. She has just brushed her teeth.

D **2.** Have you ever played baseball? / No, I've never played baseball, but I've played volleyball.

   3. Have you ever worked in a restaurant? / No, I've never worked in a restaurant, but I've worked in a library.

   4. Have you ever seen the Eiffel Tower in Paris? / No, I've never seen the Eiffel Tower in Paris, but I've seen the Taj Mahal in India.

   4. Did you eat **5.** has visited

B **2.** We bought a new car last week.

   3. Have Diane and Paul arrived yet?

   4. Have you ever been to Florida?

   5. Kelly and I have been good friends since 2005.

   6. He forgot to turn off the TV yesterday.

Learn & Practice 3

A **2.** since **3.** when **4.** since

Super Writing

A **3.** Cindy lived in Singapore for four years.

   4. Cindy has lived in Turkey since 2012.

   5. Wilson lived in Canada for ten years.

   6. Wilson has lived in England since 2009.

B **2.** When did Bob lose his job?

   3. What time did you wash your car?

   4. How long has Kimberly had her driving licence?

   5. When did Christina go out?

   6. How long has your father been in hospital?

C **3.** Eric has already scuba diving.

   4. Eric hasn't traveled around Australia yet.

   5. Eric tasted a snake two days ago.

   6. Eric has already stayed in the jungle for a week.

   7. Eric has already tried canoeing.

   8. Eric hasn't visited Egypt yet.

D **2.** Kelly has improved her Spanish since she decided to study more.

   3. Sarah hasn't gone out with her friends since she found a new job.

   4. My wife and I have known each other since we were in elementary school.

   5. I have met Alexis since I was a freshman in high school.

Unit 14
Present Perfect 3
p. 84

Learn & Practice 1

A **2.** did / do / stayed

   3. Have / finished / finished

   4. Have / been / went

Learn & Practice 2

A **2.** Have you every flown **3.** went

Unit 15
Comparison 1
p. 90

Learn & Practice 1

A **2.** the same town as **3.** similar

   4. different from

   5. the same as / different from

Learn & Practice 2

A **2.** harder than me **3.** bigger than the moon

4. prettier than her

5. more powerful than your brother

6. more popular than my boyfriend

Learn & Practice 3

A **2.** as dangerous as **3.** as intelligent as

4. as well as **5.** as hard as

Super Writing

A **2.** The train is slower than the plane.

3. The yellow car is more modern than the red car.

4. Korea is smaller than Japan.

B **2.** A golf player isn't the same height as a basketball player.

3. A soccer ball is the same shape as a volleyball.

4. An amateur athlete doesn't have the same ability as a professional athlete.

C **2.** Bob got home as late as Susan.

3. A river isn't as big as an ocean.

4. Kathy didn't study as hard as Lucy.

E **2.** House 1 and House 3 are the same. (House 1 is the same as House 3.)

3. House 1 is different from House 2. (House 1 and 2 are different.)

4. House 4 is similar to Houses 1 and 3. (House 4, 1, and 3 are similar.)

5. House 2 and House 3 are different. (House 2 is different from House 3.)

6. House 3 is not similar to House 2. (House 3 and House 2 are different.)

Unit 16
Comparison 2
p. 96

Learn & Practice 1

A **2.** alike **3.** like **4.** like

Learn & Practice 2

A **2.** the fastest / of

3. the biggest / in

4. the longest / in

5. the most interesting / of

6. the best / in

7. the largest / in

Learn & Practice 3

A **2.** one of the most famous fashion designers

3. one of the prettiest women

4. one of the most beautiful cities

5. one of the hottest days

Super Writing

A **2.** The giraffe is the tallest animal in the world.

3. The ostrich is the biggest bird in the world.

4. The Pluto is the farthest planet from the sun.

B **2.** Seoul is the most important cities in Korea.

3. The Grand Canyon is one of the most beautiful places in the world.

4. The Yangtze River is one of the longest rivers in Asia.

5. The Han River is one of the greatest historical significances of Korea.

6. A Rolls Royce is one of the most expensive cars in the world.

C **2.** Pepsi tastes like Coke. / Pepsi and Coke taste alike.

3. A football player doesn't dress like a rugby player. / A football player and a rugby player don't dress alike.

4. A Korean classroom doesn't look like a classroom in another country. / A Korean classroom and a classroom in another country don't look alike.

D **3.** Jenny is as old as Ava.

4. Alice is the shortest girl of the three.

5. Ava is the heaviest girl of the three.

6. Ava is heavier than Alice.

7. Ava is taller than Jenny.

8. Alice is the youngest girl of the three.

Unit 17
Gerunds and Infinitives 1
p. 102

Learn & Practice 1

A **2.** jogging **3.** cleaning **4.** Dancing

Learn & Practice 2

A **2.** It / to lose weight **3.** It / to save

4. It / to study

B **2.** to study **3.** traveling **4.** learning **5.** visiting

6. to come

Learn & Practice 3
A **2.** to sing / singing **3.** to play **4.** to snow / snowing

Learn & Practice 4
A **2.** to **3.** for **4.** for **5.** to

B **2.** me to call **3.** her not to drive
   4. Michelle to come **5.** me to leave

Super Writing
A **2.** It is important to exercise daily and not to skip breakfast.
   3. It is important not to eat too much of any one food.
   4. It is always interesting to hear one of your old stories.

B **2.** I hope to travel by train.
   3. Bruno wants to become a pilot.
   4. My mother often puts off washing the dishes.
   5. Kevin would like to drink orange juice.
   6. Tom avoids fighting with his brother.

C **2.** She needs to go to the bookstore to buy some books.
   3. They went to Egypt to see the ancient pyramids.
   4. They took a walk in the park to get some fresh air.

D **2.** The teacher told her to tell the truth.
   3. Olivia persuaded William to wash his feet.
   4. The doctor advised him to stop smoking.
   5. She warned us not to knock on the door loudly.
   6. Jessica invited Maria to stay at her house on Saturday night.

Unit 18
Gerunds and Infinitives 2
p. 108

Learn & Practice 1
A **2.** at **3.** working **4.** being
B **2.** went swimming **3.** goes shopping

Learn & Practice 2
A **2.** to give **3.** to get

Learn & Practice 3
A **2.** used to jog **3.** used to go
   4. is used to eating
   5. am not used to working

Learn & Practice 4
A **2.** rich enough **3.** big enough **4.** enough chairs
   5. too young **6.** too dirty

Super Writing
A **2.** He was delighted to buy a new smartphone yesterday.
   3. Were you surprised to meet your first love in Italy?
   4. Were you sad to hear the news?
   5. She was wrong to take the train without a ticket.

B **2.** Sam is too busy to go to the party.
   3. Cody has enough money to buy the ties.
   4. Peter was too tired to wash the dishes.

C **2.** wasn't used to using chopsticks / is used to using chopsticks
   3. wasn't used to working nights / is used to working nights

D **2.** like going
   3. about going

E **2.** Does Kevin like to go skydiving? / No, he doesn't. He likes to go scuba diving.

Unit 19
Conjunctions
p. 114

Learn & Practice 1
A **2.** and **3.** , but **4.** , but **5.** or **6.** (,) and

Learn & Practice 2
A **2.** , so **3.** because **4.** because **5.** , so

Learn & Practice 3
A **2.** So do I. **3.** Neither did I. **4.** Neither do I.
   5. So can I. **6.** Neither have I. **7.** So will I. **8.** So did I.

Super Writing
A **2.** It was very hot, so we opened the window.
   3. The teenage girls will go on a picnic, or (they will) go to the amusement park.
   4. Tom is foolish, but his brother is wise.
   5. My stomachache was really bad, so I took some medicine for it.
   6. I go to the restaurant because the waiter is really handsome.
   7. We didn't have class because the teacher was

absent.

8. The flight attendants served dinner, but I didn't eat.

C **2.** Ava won't go to the movies, and neither will Sophia.

3. I enjoyed my holidays very much, and so did Matt.

4. Kevin eats too much junk food, and so do you.

D **2.** my roommate does too

3. my brother doesn't either

4. pasta is too

5. anteaters don't either

6. tortoises are too

D **2.** When water reaches boiling point, it changes into steam.

3. If you throw an apple into the air, gravity pulls it back to earth again.

4. If I feel really tired, I (usually) listen to K-pop music.

E **2.** Shall I go to Korea or France? / If I were you, I'd go to Korea.

Unit 20
p. 120
Conditional Clauses

Learn & Practice 1

A **2.** tells / keep **3.** snows / wear

Learn & Practice 2

A **2.** finishes / can go

Learn & Practice 3

A **2.** had **3.** knew **4.** didn't have **5.** were

Learn & Practice 4

A **2.** I wish I knew Jenny's phone number.

3. Kelly wishes she had a smartphone.

4. We wish we were university students.

Super Writing

A **2.** I wish journalists didn't write untrue stories about me.

3. I wish moviegoers didn't touch me and pull my clothes.

4. I wish I didn't have to sign autographs all the time.

5. I wish I could go to the restaurant to get food.

6. I wish I could wear anything I wanted.

7. I wish I had privacy.

C **3.** If I lose my job, I won't find another job.

4. If I don't find another job, I'll lose my apartment.

5. If I lose my apartment, I'll move back to my parents' house.

6. If I move back to my parents' house, I'll get very bored.

7. If I get very bored, I'll go fishing every day.